Discovering God Within

Discovering God Within

John R. Yungblut

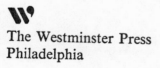

The Westminster Press
Philadelphia

Scripture quotations from the Revised Standard Version of the Bible are copyrighted 1946, 1952, © 1971, 1973 by the Division of Christian Education of the National Council of the Churches of Christ in the U.S.A., and are used by permission.

First edition

Published by The Westminster Press®
Philadelphia, Pennsylvania

PRINTED IN THE UNITED STATES OF AMERICA
9 8 7 6 5 4 3 2 1

Grateful acknowledgment is made to Harper & Row, Publishers, Inc., for permission to use excerpts from *Meister Eckhart: A Modern Translation* by Raymond Bernard Blakney. Copyright 1941 by Harper & Row, Publishers, Inc.

Library of Congress Cataloging in Publication Data

Yungblut, John R
    Discovering God within.

    Includes bibliographical references.
    1. Mysticism. I. Title.
BV5082.2.Y86   248'.22   78–21713
ISBN 0–664–24231–6

Dedicated to

Rufus Jones, who, when I sought authenticity in religion, directed me to the mystics

and to my wife, June, who taught me to seek among artists the images that reflect the authentic experience

Contents

Foreword   9

Part 1 The Mystical Way
in Christianity

Chapter I   The Point of Departure: The Meaning
                  of Religion   15

Chapter II   The Meaning of Mysticism   38

Chapter III   The Cultivation of the Mystical Faculty   55

Chapter IV   Vagaries and Aberrations of the Mystical
                  Way   74

Part 2 Some Varieties
of Christian Mysticism

Chapter V   The Fountainhead: Jesus the Jewish
                  Mystic   91

Chapter VI   The Christ-Mysticism of Paul
                  the Apostle   106

Chapter VII   The God-Mysticism of the Fourth
                  Gospel   128

Chapter VIII   The Aesthetic Mysticism of Augustine   153

Chapter IX   The Philosophical Mysticism
              of Meister Eckhart   165

Chapter X   The Material Mysticism
              of Teilhard de Chardin   178

Conclusion   193

Notes   195

Foreword

There is a certain presumption in undertaking to write a book. The admonition of Ecclesiastes should give anyone pause: "Of making many books there is no end. . . . Vanity of vanities . . .; all is vanity." Perhaps, for the lover of books, the passion to produce one more is the greatest of all vanities. In a day when there is already a multitude of books, yet another might only contribute to that malaise which Ecclesiastes called "a weariness of the flesh."

If a writer's offense against himself in assuming a public posture of vanity, and against his neighbor in contributing to weariness, fail to deflect his intention, then he must surely recoil at the potential offense against God if he aspires in his book to write of the things that are eternal! Even a Milton must tremble inwardly when he proposes to "justify the ways of God to Men." How, then, shall an ordinary person presume to interpret true religion? But if a writer be so brash as to run all three risks in their ascending gravity, he may at least hope to be forgiven the inner compulsion to give to another the best he has. Perhaps he is driven by the suspicion that, if he does not shape what is precious to him and offer it to another, it will vanish from his own mind and spirit.

That wistful self-reproach of Augustine's "O Beauty, so old and so new, too late have I loved thee!" must have found its only surcease in the disciplined attempt to point to that beauty for the benefit of his fellows through the medium of words. In enabling them to see it "in time," he may have found inner reassurance that it was not "too late" for him. Certainly one way of loving the beauty one has known is to summon another to behold it. Even the Buddha, who is said to have attained Nirvana in the renunciation of all desire, was possessed by one final desire: to lead others into the presence of the same beauty. To such a vocation he might safely devote the full passion of the manhood which had been purged of every other "attachment."

From a superficial point of view, the life of Søren Kierkegaard would seem to be one of almost unrelieved loneliness. But, in truer perspective, one imagines that Kierkegaard quite willingly forwent the idle conversation and easy sociability that satisfy most persons in order that he might communicate in depth with a chosen companion of the spirit, "that solitary one." To this imagined friend he brought, as to an altar, his richest gifts, fondly fashioned with toil and costly patience. Nor was this merely soliloquy or monologue. No child ever listened more devotedly to the comments, questions, and protestations of an imaginary playmate. Kierkegaard had sustained recollection of the presence of "that solitary one" who afforded him comfort in his own solitude. Dialogue with this constant companion, by turns antagonist and protagonist, is what gives his writing the unmistakable character of dialectic. How many of our contemporaries in this twentieth century have strangely recognized their own identity in "that solitary one," and find themselves personally addressed! What rewarding solace there must have been in the anticipation of so deep and abiding a dialogue with so many! How shall we count the number of his friends of the spirit in our day?

This book is similarly addressed to some unknown seeker who, in some deeper sense, may discover himself or herself well known and gently loved for having brought to this writing so many points of contact in those hidden places of the heart and mind whence merge what Wordsworth called, "Obstinate questionings of sense and outward things, fallings from us, vanishings." To such a one I need make no further apology. He shall be in some sense my "everyman," she my "everywoman." All others would be well advised to ascertain quite early that what is here set forth does not speak to their condition and, turning swiftly away, spare themselves the unnecessary weariness.

I would venture a further word of gratitude to those who discover as these pages are read some kinship with the author. They may indeed be closer to me than a blood brother or sister. The ceaseless dialogue in the author's experience over some thirty years with other writers, with teachers and friends, implicit in the narrow path or way which is here set forth, may quicken recollections of a similar turn or bond or recovery in the reader's experience.

The inwardly exclaimed "Hallelujah" or "Amen" will not be heard with that immediate reassurance which is the gracious gift of some congregations to their preachers, nor that more subtle mist of which Joseph Fort Newton wrote in his autobiography as returning from the pew in response to the gentle rain which descends from the pulpit. Yet, in the strange economy of the spirit, there can be a communion no less real than that provoked by the spoken word. The "monstrance" of the Word does not require a pulpit or high altar in an established parish church. Where it is present, by God's grace, there is communion from the depths of one being to another. And one who is privileged to minister in this hidden way is twice blessed by those who hear: once in the silent audience of the reader's more interior attention, and again in the direct confirmation which may be made known only in eternity, but beckons, even now, in hope and promise.

Thomas Kelly spoke of "knowing another in the things that are eternal." This kind of knowing can take place in some measure even through the medium of a book. I aspire to speak directly to the interior being of thoughtful Christian leaders, both clergy and lay. It is my concern, through this "radial" meeting, so to interpret and advocate the mystical strain in our great heritage that individuals, here and there, one by one, may be persuaded to pursue the cultivation of the mystical or contemplative faculty in themselves and to become, within the sphere of their influence, evangelists on behalf of the mystical way forward for the church.

J.R.Y.

Part 1

The Mystical Way in Christianity

Chapter I

The Point of Departure: The Meaning of Religion

The purpose of this book is to interpret and to advocate the mystical approach to religious experience. No approach could be more "catholic." It can lay claim to being at once universal and immemorial, not merely within Christendom but within the continuum of all living religions. Moreover, the first and last "protest-ants" in every great tradition are likely to be numbered among the mystics. Aldous Huxley has drawn impressive brief for the argument of "catholicity," baptizing this ever new born infant in every great religion "the perennial philosophy." Raymond B. Blakney in the introduction to his modern translation of an anthology of the writings of the celebrated fourteenth-century mystic, Meister Eckhart, substantiates our second claim, at least with reference to the history of Christianity, in these words:

> The Reformation can be traced back to Eckhart spiritually and intellectually—if not ecclesiastically. There was enough matter for any reformation to work on in what Eckhart said plainly to whoever would listen to him. He could not be satisfied until he had made certain of the creative, ultimate source of all being, in the only place where it can be immediately known: in the depths of the immaterial self of a man. This is Protestantism.[1]

But I would not press this line of argument. "Catholic" and "Protestant" are words with a special connotation for Christendom. I want to set what I have to say in a still larger context. I believe that the time has come when ecumenicity itself, great and important as it is, does not venture forth far enough. Here will be renewed the claim that others have made that mysticism is indeed the language of communication between the living religions because it is the heart and core of all true religion. I want to present mysticism as constituting an authentic apostolic succession within historic Christianity and as affording an opportunity for dialogue at this juncture with other religions that have a like succession, including religious humanism.

TOWARD AN INTERFAITH DEFINITION OF RELIGION

That Which Binds Together in One Bundle

Before I undertake to define what I shall mean by mysticism, I want to make clear what I shall mean by the word "religion" itself. Of course I shall use the word with different connotations at different times. I have already used it with reference to the organic complex of the historic faiths in referring to the living religions. I might well use it in denoting the present institutionalized forms of these faiths which vary so enormously within a single tradition. But, at the outset, it is fair to inquire what presuppositions lie behind my use of the word in its more general connotation.

There are two striking definitions of religion in the Bible. One appears in The Book of Micah: "What does the Lord require of you but to do justice, and to love kindness, and to walk humbly with your God?" (Micah 6:8). The second is set forth in The Letter of James: "Religion that is pure and undefiled before God and the Father is this: to visit orphans and widows in their affliction, and to keep oneself unstained from the world" (James 1:27). Though the first is prophetic and poetic, and the other more priestly and specific, both formulas embody the same principles. Both have sacramental significance in that they point to outward and visible signs and insist at the same time on an inward and spiritual grace. "To do justice, and to love kindness" is, in practice, to be the kind of person who does not neglect "to visit orphans and widows in their affliction." "To walk humbly with . . . God" requires the interior processes of purging, gatheredness, and recollection that alone can keep one "unstained from the world." Here is the prophet's passion for social reform rightly fused with the psalmist's interior posture of devotion. The same marriage of outward deportment with inward quest for purity would be characteristic of the noblest of the mystics in other great traditions.

These definitions vividly illustrate the chief point I should like to make about the nature of religion in its most characteristic and developed form. The word itself, in its very derivation, suggests the most profound insight: *religio* comes from a verb meaning "to bind together." Religion, then, is that inner imperative which compels a person to bind everything together in some harmonious whole. It is the compulsion to find one's own myth of meaning. One finds oneself constrained to pursue this inescapable vocation, not only in the chaotic complexity of that interior world which modern depth psychology has revealed but also in the anarchy reflected in human relations in their present state. It is even found in the apparent purposelessness of much that one beholds in environing nature. Religion is ultimately what an individual makes of these two worlds in their interrelationship and togetherness: the microcosm of the interior self, as one experiences this evermore deepening maze, and the macrocosm of the expanding universe in which we find ourselves mysteriously placed as both a part of and as somehow "over against." Even the testimony that some contemporary literary artists perceive only ultimate meaninglessness reveals unwittingly the religious instinct unconsciously at work, reporting, at least, a "consistent" pattern.

The religious faculty is the most comprehensive and therefore, normally, the most imperious. Freud and his successors have taught us how pervasive is the sexual instinct. Its repression has been advanced as plausible motivating power for the building of civilization itself. Its infinite permutations lend credence to the analyst's reconstructions of the origins of the neurotic patterns in earliest childhood. One is almost persuaded to look for all unaccountable motivations in the area of some unconscious sexual stimulus. Its basic importance has been established beyond dispute. We simply acknowledge the relative dominance of this instinct in order to emphasize that the religious instinct, and we are persuaded that is what it ought rightly to be called, is yet more potent, when it is properly released and realized. Its purview, since it is all-inclusive, contains the sexual along with everything else, while the converse cannot be claimed.

Religion by its very nature is constrained to find a proper place for the sexual in its pattern of wholeness. The sexual instinct, despite its constant and clamorous claims, is not similarly impelled to find a place in its scheme for everything else, including religious need. Unchecked, the sexual drive can quite ruthlessly bend fact, reason, memory, will, to its fulfillment, or rather to the ever unfulfilled satiety of its consuming passion. But it does not characteristically construct a world view of its own that can enthrall the more quiet and reflective moods of humankind. Our generation may be the first to give just recognition to the ubiquity in human relations of the sexual and its derivatives. But we must confess that there is a still more comprehensive faculty. It involves a passion to make sense of the world: it first inspires us with a perception of potential harmony, and then constrains us to seek its realization.

Perhaps here is to be sought the source of the strange rivalry, and still stranger affinity, these two instincts bear toward each other. The second most potent human proclivity, this sexual urge, might be expected now and again to make pretensions to the throne. That which claims so great a part of our conscious and unconscious attention is quite often associated with the enveloping and absorbing need to perceive and to create a unity on every level of human awareness. Literature attests the range of this association, from degenerate figures who can engage in detached sexual stimulation and mindless "religious" expression at the same time, to Dante's epic song which can combine at once a storming of the very gates of heaven with a troubador's lyric to his beloved. Elmer Gantry, however much of a charlatan Sinclair Lewis intended him to be, has been convincingly portrayed in drama as deceiving himself as well as his congregations in the degree of interpenetration of sexual passion and religious fervor. The same is true of the confession of the evangelist in the film *Marjoe.* But when Solomon's Song of Songs was proven to be an early poem about the way of a man with a maid in the purity and passion of human love, it seemed an appropriate image for a Love that never palls and a divine Lover who never betrays. Those mystics who have not recoiled from sexual imagery in speaking of the divine-human marriage have always known of this relationship. The only leverage that could release an Augustine from bondage to the sensual was a passion that sought to make of the sundered parts of his nature one sound and exquisite whole. The sexual could be subdued only by a new "embracement," sweeter far than any afforded by the arms of a lover.

C. G. Jung has reminded us that for more than fifty years we have known that the human being is "duplex" rather than "simplex," that there is an unconscious dimension to the human psyche far more vast than the conscious. There is operative in the unconscious a shadow side of the conscious personality, often contradictory in nature, representing repressed and compensatory aspects of the psyche. The religious impulse is just awakening to an enormous new task: that of undertaking a reconciliation of the content of the conscious with that of the unconscious. From the religious point of view the objective is wholeness, a conscious recognition of all the elements at work in the unconscious and a reworking of the personality in the direction of integration. "Individuation" is the name that Jung gave to this process. Beyond the split between the ego consciousness and the shadow in the unconscious lies the promise of a union of opposites in the self. Jung has said that the archetype for the self and the archetype for God are ultimately indistinguishable. So when religion is authentic, it seeks wholeness. Its processes of revelation in every great tradition attest that the very nature of sin is the tendency of some aspect of life to seize the reins and pretend to be the whole. Unhappily, the major religions, notably the various sects within them, frequently have stifled this genius of religion. As Arnold Toynbee has pointed out, the tragedy of Judaism, inherited in turn by Christianity and Islam, has been its proclivity for exclusiveness. Religion, in its purest form, is itself man's messiah. But when, in the name of religion, religions confer messiahship on a people or a person, and then disparage other peoples or other religions that do not accept a particular reconstruction of history, or when within Christendom one part of the body informs the rest of the body that it possesses the whole truth, the spirit of religion has vanished. The salt has altogether lost its savor.

The poet need not have been so vague in his allusion: it is precisely the religious instinct "that doesn't love a wall, that wants it down." What irony, then, that in the name of religion we should have erected so many walls, until what is normally called secular assumes the role that was religion's rightful prerogative! But those who have known the fragrance of the rose care not what it is called so long as its fragrance remains. In our day, this unmistakable fragrance is often to be detected where no creed is recited, no kerygma preached, no ritual practiced: some existential community in which men and women are finding that it is indeed "good and pleasant . . . when brothers dwell in unity." Much has been made of the "scandal" of particularity which the Christian faith posits for the world. On the other hand, here is a strange "scandal" with which the world confronts the church: the spectacle of a kind of bondedness, koinonia if you will, entirely detached from the sphere of organized institutional religion. Some have found, at least temporarily, a viable substitute for religion in our day by participation in the civil rights and peace movements, in a space project team, in medical or scientific research, or in a commune devoted to simple living.

There might well be forms of true religion, possessing the authentic quality I have been describing, in which participants refrain even from using the name of God. Sick of the all but incurable predilection for attempting to use God for our own purposes, confused and annoyed by the associations and attributes the various theologies have attached to the word, some of our contemporaries have decided to abandon the use of the word and to relinquish traditional dependence upon a personal Being with omniscience, who is held to be at once all-loving and all-powerful. For some this may mean that the God progressively proclaimed in much of our Judeo-Christian heritage is dead in the sense of a being whom they can reverence or obey. Such reticence may be close to the holy silence of those first Hebrews who would not speak the name of God lest they be stricken dead, and to those authentic "Israelites" of every time and place who steadfastly refuse to "image" God. After all, the universal testimony of the greatest mystics in every religion is that God is, and must remain, imageless. Did not Pascal rightly insist that "every religion that does not affirm that God is hidden is not true"? In this one important respect, the posture of some modern philosophers and literary artists would appear to be closer to the truth about God than some boisterous and blatant churches.

Some years ago a devout churchman at a college faculty colloquy was heard to ask somewhat plaintively of his colleagues, "Is there any apology for theism that can win the respectful attention of the unchurched intellectuals of our day?" I should not know how to answer that query in the affirmative, since theism itself implies the existence of a personal, transcendent God revealed within the Judeo-Christian historical continuity, and it is precisely these revelations as traditionally represented that are called into question by the nonbeliever. But it is my passionate conviction that there is an apology for "religion," as distinct from "theism," that can win the respectful attention of many philosophers, scientists, and artists who reject the institutional churches today. This apology will take the shape of an advocacy of that form of religion known as mysticism.

A Sustained Pursuit of Perfection

The peculiar province of the religious instinct is a divinely creative one. It perceives potential form in the void, brings order out of chaos, and searches out the hidden potential for more productive relatedness in every society. It strives to realize ever purer harmonies in personal relationships, in communities of otherness, in human society. This passion, like the lesser ones, can be perverted, as when fascism or communism with "religious" zeal pursues ruthlessly the imagined harmony of some conceptualized utopia. No social reconstruction can reflect the authentic religious motivation which leaves out of its projected whole any of the parts or looks upon any segment of humankind as having inherently less worth than any other. Only that which in its relentless pursuit of order and harmony reaches unerringly for the highest and noblest and most inclusive in any given potential is truly religious.

Lest what I am calling the religious instinct be identified as what in some schools of psychology is known as the superego (though there are obvious similarities of function), I must isolate and designate still more characteristics of the religious faculty in man. The ethical is essential in the human sphere of reference, since inclusive harmony presupposes the basis of morality. We would do well to recall William James's prescription: "There must be something at once solemn, serious, and tender about any attitude we call religious." Solemn, because there is intuitive response to what Rudolf Otto called the *mysterium tremendum.* Serious, because there is profound recognition of a built-in moral imperative to incarnate, in the spirit of individuals and human institutions, a glory the imagination envisions. Tender, because there appears to be a natural affinity between the aspiration which seeks more beautiful harmonies in human relations and a capacity for altruistic love that makes itself known in goodwill fused with gentleness.

This persistent motivation to bind apparently disparate things together in some pattern of wholeness falls short of the authentically religious when it is content with less than a sustained pursuit of perfection. Even without a distinctly delineated image of perfection, such as a code of conduct inherited in the canon of religious precept, or living myths which reflect the character of the messiah or guru, persons are yet beguiled by a vague but persistent inward vision of what ought to be. Nor can they be dissuaded from the hope that what ought to be might be if certain conditions were met in the outward behavior and the hidden inward attitude of the self in those who constitute a given society. The vision of the Eternal City promises always to become the Kingdom of God on earth.

To suggest that such striving is the result of a guilt complex arising out of known failure to meet the prescribed standards of the particular religion or culture in which they have been raised is to beg the question. One must yet inquire into the ultimate source of this yearning for purity and holiness in those who first conceived and articulated the demands. They could have secured no hold upon the conscience of another without some substantiation by some interior monitor in that other. Jesus reminded his disciples that they could not know what manner of man he was unless the Father inwardly revealed this knowledge to them. What one intuitively recognizes as true and beautiful and good does not arise solely out of what has been taught, but from that mysterious monitor, the center of one's value judgments, which may often find itself in rebellion against what has been taught. The religious instinct both to be whole and to help create wholeness in one's total environment has therefore larger reference and more vast significance than what is usually implied by the psychological term "superego."

Two questions pursue reflective men and women in every culture: In what does true manhood or womanhood consist? and, What would real community be like? All noble theologies and philosophies have taken their impetus from the attempt to make plausible reply to these two questions out of deep longings and aspirations. Here the inner light is most characteristically at work. In the fullness of its promise, it is quite clearly a "light that never was, on sea or land." Human beings have the peculiar faculty of dreaming of an adulthood they are not capable of living, and of imagining a society they have not experienced. More than that, they have the capacity of hitching their wayward little wagons to this strange star whose light shines only in the immaterial firmament of the mind, and of drawing themselves by the might and main of prayer and deed a little closer to what may ever finally elude them.

A Holy Spirit at Work at All Times and in All Cultures

Some of the living religions of our day have proven their greatness by surviving the ravages of time. They have surmounted the limitations of space through successful transplantation into cultures in which they did not arise. These religions

have given a name to that source or author of the values they
have discovered and explored in the process of attempting to
answer these two questions: What would it be like to be a good
man or woman? and, What kind of society would such persons
build? That name is variously God, Brahma, the Absolute, the
One. The answers that have been given to these perennial questions by certain mystics in the living religions bear so striking
a resemblance to one another that we may safely infer that the
processes of reason and intuition of those standing within these
different traditions are informed by the same ultimate reality.
Christians may explain this fact by saying that the Holy Spirit
(God within) has been at work at all times and in all places.
Hindus and Buddhists might say the Atman reveals his identity
to be one in whomsoever he resides. A Jungian psychologist
would say that the archetype of the self or God in the collective
unconscious produces the same archetypal images in all persons.

Human beings find themselves constrained to "body forth"
this vision in images, metaphors, and myths, because it is the
only way they know to hold on to its fleeting beauty which more
enthralls them in exalted moments of interior illumination than
any material object their senses have known. Later generations
freeze these images, metaphors, and myths into theological dogmas with interlocking systems by the exercise of logic, once the
premises have been accepted "by faith." Graven images continue to be recognized as idols, and reverence for them as idolatry. But the verbal images constructed by the mind and wrought
into creeds, confessions of faith, and rigid theological systems
are not recognized as the idols, nor their vain repetition as the
idolatry, they really are.

When shall we learn that the primary responsibility of religious education is not to propagate the notion that these images,
metaphors, and myths are literally true? Rather, it must spend
its energies upon inculcating in children a sustained capacity to
distinguish between shadow and substance, symbol and reality,
means and end, doctrine about and experience of deity, sacrament, and grace. Some grown men and women never learn the
distinction. Too many of us have to undergo an intensely lonely

and extremely painful struggle over many years to free ourselves from this inherited and carefully cultivated idolatry.

With this mental reservation clearly stated, I want to insist upon the wisdom of the continued use of the word symbol "God" in our Western culture, with its Judeo-Christian heritage. It means that ultimate reality to which or to whom we attribute both the source and the vitality of our triumvirate of values: beauty, truth, and goodness. To man's conception of this ultimate reality, even within the Judeo-Christian tradition, have been attached historically many characteristics. Some of these are conflicting and mutually contradictory within the pages of the Bible, not to speak of the multiplied confusion in man's subsequent spiritual pilgrimage in the West. But I would venture to suggest that among persons of goodwill there has been a progress toward consensus concerning the prevailing attribute: that energizing agape love whose will is itself goodness and whose form is the highest beauty and the ultimate truth about our universe. Whenever and wherever any other hierarchy of values has been erected by segments of the church, placing something else at the apex (i.e., power or legalistic justice), there has been stasis or retrogression. Even time has displayed no power to make this ancient good uncouth. And when, as in this present time, people have lost the "scent" of God, is it not because they have been beguiled by some other presumed attribute or been denied the possibility in our world of experiencing at first hand this kind of love? This is not to say that the archetype, God, or Godhead, does not in some mysterious sense also encompass evil. This will be discussed later.

It is foolish and futile to forgo the use of a symbol so hallowed by time on the ground that this would free us once and for all from false and even demonic images often associated with it. The accumulated interior attitudes of reverence, awe, creatureliness, and devotion that the word "God" evokes are not readily transferred to some new word. Granted the old word has borne in many a mind an unhappy freight from which it can be wrested perhaps only by the individual's "willing" and exultantly "proclaiming" the "death of God"! It is a poor bargain. To begin the religious quest *de novo* with some new symbol is a vain attempt. To create an individually circumscribed concept may remove certain false associations and connotations of the ancient name. At the same time, it would be a great loss to forgo the incalculable accumulated treasure in that symbol which still speaks to the deepest and highest in the human heart, and continues for so many unfailingly to ring the sanctus bell in the hidden chancel of conscience and aspiration. When the purpose is to name the Unnamable, is not one name as good as another? What infinite advantage, then, in staying with a name so inextricably interwoven in the writings—theological, aesthetic, and devotional—and the liturgies we have inherited from that vast succession of those who have loved the Unnamable.

Of course we shall have to purge the symbol of its historical masculine connotation. While it is wiser to retain a personal rather than an impersonal pronoun with reference to God because only a person can express the divine attributes, we must always remember that God, to be God, must transcend every image, including the sexual. We shall use masculine pronouns rather than impersonal ones and rather than artificially choose feminine ones to compensate, but the reader will understand that my consciousness has been appropriately raised.

In some sense everyone's God is unique. The symbol represents what one has fashioned, in the mystery of individuality, from what one has been told of the nature of God, what one has suffered, and what one has learned from the institutional church, and from experience and reflection in the light of all this. Exodus, with unerring insight, speaks not of the God of Abraham, Isaac, and Jacob, but of "the God of Abraham, the God of Isaac, and the God of Jacob," referring to one reality quite variously known. I shall be considering primarily the God whom the greatest of the mystics have known, since by certain criteria he can be distinguished from the God of the ritualists, the institutionalists, the fundamentalists or literalists, the dualists and the dogmatic theologians. More precisely, we will still have to distinguish, at least by inference, between the God of Augustine, the God of Eckhart, and the God of Teilhard de Chardin.

TOWARD AN EVOLVING CONCEPT OF GOD THROUGH MYTH AND METAPHOR

The definition of the nature of religion with which I began requires a new perspective in theology. It must take cognizance of, and be related harmoniously to, a philosophy, a cosmology, an ecology, a paleontology, an anthropology, a sociology, and a psychology that would be viable for our time. During the period of history spanned in the writings of the Bible, people found that their earlier concepts of God were too small to encompass the later visions, experiences, and revelations. I have accepted as an axiom in my position that revelation did not cease with the New Testament. Man's concept of God and of himself must evolve, or he is destined to stagnation, if not retrogression.

Image-making, metaphor-building, mythologizing are inescapable practices prompted by the religious instinct. Demythologize we must as an expanding horizon reduces or destroys the value of a particular myth by revealing that it is inadequate, misleading, or false. But let us not deceive ourselves. In religion we demythologize but to remythologize. If we were not to do so, we might retain a philosophy but not a religion. As well compose poetry without imagery! Two things are of the utmost importance: that we never cease to reexamine every myth to determine whether it is still a viable symbol of an aspect of reality which we experience or are in contact with by the inference of the mind, since our understanding of the environing universe and of ourselves changes and evolves; and that we constantly recollect that myths are myths, and do not fail to distinguish between the reality and the symbol.

Endless confusion has been caused, in my judgment, by Rudolf Bultmann's demand that we demythologize the cosmology of the Bible while he refuses to distinguish between myth and reality regarding the "kerygma," the kernel of doctrine about Jesus in the New Testament. He insists that our scientific perspective requires that we move beyond the notion of a three-storied universe. But does not this very same scientific perspective of our age demand that we remythologize the resurrection, for example, at least to the point of disallowing any causal relationship between an empty tomb and the disciples' experience of the resurrection? Can we apply a standard of truth in one area of human experience and not in another? Does not the central characteristic of true religion—that is, to bind everything into one bundle—compel us just at this point to keep our universe one? Must we not therefore insist that it is not only untenable but fundamentally immoral and irreligious to imply that "to the eyes of faith" something can be literally true which violates the very principle to which scientific observation is dedicated?

A certain professor of theology (in the days before women attended seminaries), when pressed with questions regarding the virgin birth or a flesh-and-bones resurrection, said to his students: "But, gentlemen, *something* happened." To make no further claim is to preserve the religious grace of restoring a myth to its rightful status—as a myth. It is possible that at least some of those who participated in the original shaping of these myths knew what they were doing. Undoubtedly something both psychically and psychologically of profound importance happened to Mary in the months preceding her conception of Jesus, and during the ensuing period through his birth.

The associated myth of the Annunciation, for example, reexamined in the light both of its contemporary Jewish context of hope and aspiration and of its timeless psychological insight, still has the ring of reality. Caryll Houselander, in her book *The Reed of God,* rehearses devotionally the wonder of the acceptable aspects of the "miracle." In language that continues to give the myth of the virgin birth some coinage value in our day she states: "Mary's virginity consisted in her self-emptying that she might be filled with the spirit of God." Asserting the mystic's poetic license, she manages to give an ancient myth new lease on life: "What happened to Mary is precisely what is to happen to each one of us: The Holy Spirit is to conceive the Christ-life in us."

Unhappily, the still fluid substance of the myth had not even found its way into the pages of the New Testament before the literalists and legalists had greatly impaired its value. By asserting that Mary had not "known" Joseph, they at once implied the intervention of a supernatural factor and a fixed relationship between sexual union and sin. Literalists ever since, who have been unwilling or unable to distinguish between myth and reality, have either applied the principle of that rare biological phenomenon among insects, crustaceans, and worms known as parthenogenesis or removed the virgin birth from the realm of argument altogether by insisting that "to the eyes of faith," at least, it happened literally as stated.

"Gentlemen, *something* happened!" Enthusiastically agreed. Something did happen, something that has not ceased to shake the world. But we had better delineate carefully what we mean by the myth in our twentieth century, as Caryll Houselander attempts to do for herself and others. Next we must make sure that our children do not misunderstand us and mistake our new version of the myth for the particular reality it is seeking to express.

With regard to the resurrection, once again some remythologizing is necessary to come by a form of the myth which individuals who want to keep their reasoning process whole may accept. Again, something happened! Something so phenomenal, so soul-transforming happened that we are prepared to accept at face value Paul's considered judgment: "If there is no resurrection of the dead [at least mythologically], . . . we are of all men most to be pitied." Certainly, had there been no resurrection *experience,* there would have been no Christian church, with all that this has meant on the positive side for subsequent history. But our very first religious responsibility is to disengage this myth once and for all from its literalist entanglements. Again, unhappily, before the myth entered the written account in the New Testament the literalists had made the fatal associations between the reality and specific evidence purporting to attest it: an empty tomb, a beach breakfast prepared and served by Jesus, and an invitation to Thomas to thrust his hand into the wounds. We are spared any claim that Thomas' faith was restored by responding to the invitation to do so.

Certainly, any person whose mind breathes an atmosphere

purged by the spirit of pure science in our day, who would be true to the spirit of religion as we have delineated it, must demythologize, or more accurately remythologize, the New Testament *here,* no less than in its archaic cosmology. This need not mean that we must forgo in any form the myth of the resurrection. Indeed, I am persuaded we should not, and in one sense cannot, unless and until a more viable myth emerges to reflect the reality the ancient myth symbolizes. Behind the myth lie two perennial human needs which no other myth has yet satisfied so well. These two needs are no less insistent in their demands upon us than they were for the disciples. The first is a need to affirm what only the gossamer stuff of intimations as yet commends to reason, namely, some form of survival beyond death for the experienced entity of human individuality and personality. The second is a need to affirm that the spirit that was in Jesus is ultimately victorious, though it meet here and now with crucifixion; that this love which emerged at long last in and through nature will yet redeem all nature, including human nature.

Something happened! The disciples, individually and corporately, underwent experiences that gave them such assurance of the survival of death by the person of Jesus that they gave the rest of their lives to proclaiming the resurrection and the assurance of life everlasting for the faithful. It was not merely that something happened to them which was so fully persuasive that they were never to experience sustained doubt again, but that their conviction empowered them to undertake a moral and spiritual revolution, the end of which is not yet. Something happened. Something indeed!

The mystic who wrote the Fourth Gospel, which bears the name of John, had the poetic insight to have Jesus say of himself: "I am the resurrection and the life; he who believes in me, though he die, yet shall he live, and whoever lives and believes in me shall never die." Note that these words were said to have been spoken *before* the crucifixion. The implication is clear: it was the quality of Jesus' earthly life that constitutes the "survival value" and opens the door to eternity. This suggestion lifts the myth above its unfortunate accouterments in the rest of the story and frees it for continued usefulness. But, once again, we must be clear as to the sense in which we shall understand and affirm this myth of the resurrection. Let us never forget in the name of true religion that it is and shall remain a myth— channeling to our poor, limited minds, as a sacrament, an as yet ineffable reality. The Easter morning experience of the disciples can continue to serve us as a myth, symbolizing this reality which tends to find answering confirmation in our own intima- tions as we reflect upon the two basic human needs that confront us as much as the disciples.

Some years ago a bishop of the Anglican Communion, John A. T. Robinson, charged with responsibility as "a defender of the faith," made public confession of his own interior struggle with this problem of distinguishing between myth and reality. He declared his readiness to forgo time-honored myths that no longer serve their function effectively because of the acquisition of new knowledge and changing perspectives. Christians are proverbially reluctant to subject these myths to fresh scrutiny, because they have too often directed reverence toward the sym- bols themselves. Ever since Galileo, certain cosmological sym- bols in the Bible have stood under the judgment of a changing perspective that was patently more accurate. A God whose dwelling place was "up there" had gradually been replaced by One who reigned from "out there."

From one point of view, Bishop Robinson appeared to be a little late in catching up with astronomical and philosophical developments. Still, it was commendable that he should risk his reputation with his peers as well as his superiors by setting forth in so ingenuous and disarming a way his doubts as well as his convictions. In this struggle to find mythological expression for the locus of God, the bishop was later led to accept Christian mysticism, finding the transcendence as well as the immanence of God symbolized, with proper elucidation, "in here." Wary of the historical vagaries of mysticism, with which we must come to terms in a later chapter, he first settled for Tillich's metaphor, "the ground of our being." More recently, in *Exploration Into God,* he moved to a position beyond theism, namely, panenthe- ism, that of Christian mysticism. In this way Bishop Robinson has made his intellectual peace with one of the great revolutionary changes in our perspective on the nature of space and our posture within it.

THE NEW LIGHT THAT ILLUMINATES ALL FACTS: EVOLUTION

There has been another revolution in our perspective. Some thinkers, like Julian Huxley, have thought it the greatest since the dawn of history. This change, not yet a century old, refers to our understanding of our posture within time. Since space and time are not unrelated, some have referred to the space-time continuum. The theory of evolution, informed by the science of paleontology, has been accepted in our time by intellectuals as indisputable fact. This fact has not yet been fully assimilated by theology. This new perspective on what and who we are demands more radical reconstruction of the traditional myths of Creation, the Fall, the Incarnation, the Atonement, and the Resurrection than they have yet received. Perhaps no one has come closer to suggesting the general outlines in which these radical revisions may be made than the twentieth-century Roman Catholic mystic, Pierre Teilhard de Chardin. As one who was both a highly trained scientist (in biology and paleontology) and "a defender of the faith," he recognized that the whole structure of Christian mythology had to be reworked in the light of the process of evolution and its implications. He stated clearly the moral responsibility of the theologian in our time:

> Blind indeed are those who do not see the sweep of a movement whose orbit infinitely transcends the natural sciences and has successively invaded and conquered the surrounding territory—chemistry, physics, sociology and even mathematics and the history of religions. One after the other all the fields of human knowledge have been shaken and carried away by the same under-water current in the direction of the study of some development. Is evolution a theory, a system or a hypothesis? It is much more: it is a general condition to which all theories, all hypotheses, all systems must bow and which they must satisfy henceforward if they are to be thinkable

and true. Evolution is a light illuminating all facts, a curve that all lines must follow.[2]

It is my conviction that Teilhard arrived at an extraordinary synthesis of thought, advancing the process of relating integrally the relevant findings of scientific exploration and knowledge to the traditional Christian myths. For the Roman Church some think it may come to represent the greatest synthesis since Thomas Aquinas. Perhaps, as another has proposed, referring to its poetic and unsystematic aspects, the thought of Teilhard will play Abelard to someone else's Aquinas.

Teilhard was able to win this integration of thought as man of science and man of faith because his approach to religious experience is basically mystical. He was able to take the dogmas to which he had to subscribe as a Jesuit priest and to begin to remythologize them in such a manner as to preserve their continuing value as symbols of reality. Nevertheless, in the process, the myth of Creation is transformed. That of the Fall has been so radically reworked that his position with regard to the source and nature of sin was sufficient of itself to arouse suspicions of heresy and to prompt a Roman interdict against the publication of his work during his lifetime. The doctrines of the Incarnation, the Atonement, and the Resurrection assume cosmic proportions which only his perspective of a continuing evolution of the entire universe could have imparted to them. In keeping with this scale of observation, Teilhard's Christology is more exalted than any within the history of Christian theology since Paul. Indeed, the "point omega" of the evolving universe is its eventual "Christification," as Teilhard conceives it.

There has always been a tacit, if not open, conflict between historian and theologian within the Christian ethos which comes particularly to light in their different approaches to the study of the life of Jesus. Historians pursue their discipline in the spirit of modern science, content to commit themselves to the process of induction from the facts, as far as these can be known. Traditional theologians, on the other hand, begin with the given premises of their theological commitment and proceed to deduce theories of history from chosen facts or acts of faith.

Teilhard managed to be both historian and theologian at once. As historian he took for his province not the period of recorded human events, alone, but the history of the cosmos itself, as far as this can be discerned in theories of the genesis of this planet as well as the more specific recordings of the strata in fossil remains. He approached this study in the spirit of pure science despite his theological commitment. He was able to do this because this commitment was not an uncritical, intellectual affirmation of a set of dogmas to which he believed a fixed form had been given once and for all. The commitment was to an inward experience of the love that was in Jesus as constituting the "divine milieu" in which all physical phenomena cohere as a total environment, and from which, as a center, they continue to evolve toward a "point omega." Doctrines are myths. They too are subject to this process of evolution and must be transmuted into many forms along with all things, living and inanimate. I believe that in certain areas, as in the dogmas of the Virgin Birth and the Resurrection, he did not make explicit the conclusions toward which his approach implicitly pointed—for whatever reason. But the unmistakable marks of the classical mystical approach are there, revealing the basic lines that the remythologizing must take to follow the curve of the new evolutionary perspective.

The history of mysticism in this century has been studied and scrutinized with great care by a small company of researchers. Although they worked separately, they reached remarkable concurrence in their judgment as to what was wheat and what was chaff in mystical literature; what constitutes the essence of mysticism and what its vagaries. They have isolated the element itself. They have distinguished between the unalloyed, refined reality and those unfortunate manifestations, attitudes, and emphases which have too often accompanied the real thing. No word in the history of religions has been so abused as the word "mysticism," nor has any produced such confused connotations. Yet we cannot abandon its use in favor of some new and untried symbol. There is far too profound an investment of human toil and striving in the ancient word.

SOUND RELIGIOUS EDUCATION: EDUCATION BY METAPHOR

I have noted that insights into the nature of reality which begin unashamedly as myths have a way of congealing into doctrines which are understood later as representing literal facts. We must begin our inquiry by a process of unlearning. We must enter into what may appear an unfamiliar and therefore threatening "cloud of unknowing." The principle of propaganda —i.e., if something is repeated often enough there will no longer be any serious inquiry as to its strict veracity—is unhappily pertinent here. We Christians have repeated so much about God and about his mighty acts in history, especially the myth of what we have been taught was his greatest act, the incarnation, that we have come to think of God literally as a manlike being who stands over against his universe. When he created it he saw that it was very good. But there came a time when he saw that it was so very bad he had to enter into history as a man through his "only begotten Son," that he might remake this world.

In our process of "unknowing," we must recollect the Biblical injunction that "no one has ever seen God." The only intimations we have ever had of God's very existence are the presence of values, longings, and aspirations which have emerged out of the expanding, unfolding, and evolving consciousness of living persons. The very existence of God is a projection of a hypothesis from the minds of men and women as they reflect upon the meaning of life and as they look attentively at qualities that have found expression in themselves and others—above all, for Christians, in Jesus of Nazareth. There is a sense in which the positive inference from Freud's insight is profoundly true: the Judeo-Christian God *is* a projection on the countenance of the universe of the best that human experience has known of the tender, selfless, undiscourageable love of a good father for his child. We need no further commendation of Jesus' relationship to his human father than that this epithet was his chosen name for God. He deliberately reflected the central characteristic of this God in what we mistakenly call the parable of the prodigal son instead of the parable of the father-God. Because of the inescapable power of word association, rejection by one's human father stands as the most formidable block to accepting the symbol "God" as representing ultimate value. Thereafter an additional burden rests upon every other means of grace.

Perhaps no interior emotion is so enshrined with a self-authenticating aura of the "holy" as this particular form of human love at its best. Transmuted from the particular to the universal, this love becomes the theme of Paul's lyric poetry in I Corinthians 13. This reality, more of hope than of realization, is one of our names for the Unnamable. This God of love is not "dead," nor is the symbol of his "being" archaic or meaningless. Yes, emphatically, this is a projection from the human mind. This explains whence the idea came, but does not explain away the idea, nor should it be allowed to disparage its potency. Before it was projected onto the countenance of ultimate reality in the universe from the human mind, it was mysteriously projected into the "withinness" of molecular substance, out of which emerged at length cellular substance, and, in the fullness of time, the human mind. And projected beyond the human mind on a hypothetical being named God, projected from a beginning upon an end, both wholly enshrouded in mystery, this dream of life draws us forward as to an unattained vision. It also "thrusts" us forward, from within the very ground of our being, and attests both the immanence and the transcendence of this God. Hence, while mysticism is the final ground of defense for some currently acceptable myth of theism, it is also the most thoroughgoing humanism. William Blake has put it in verse:

The Worship of God is honouring his gifts
In other men and loving the greatest men best, each according
To his Genius which is the Holy Ghost in Man; there is no other
God than that God who is the intellectual fountain of
    Humanity.[3]

Hence our point of departure for this apology for mysticism requires acceptance of two presuppositions that partake of the nature of insights rather than propositions that can be proven by logic. The first is that religion is that human impulse or instinct which compels us to try to make sense of our environing universe and to strive inwardly toward that purity of heart which is to will one thing: the good. We give the name "religion" to the mysterious motivation in us that constrains us to find or to construct order out of the environing chaos without and the still more terrifying "formlessness" within—and this around what we conceive to be "the highest," that having ultimate value. Secondly, in the process of pursuing this preoccupation in all that we are and do the religious resort to the creation of myths that are the constructs of our imagination, to which we entrust the responsibility of "bodying forth" the otherwise ineffable stuff of our aspirations.

Robert Frost once said that all sound education, save mathematical (and even this exception might be called into question), is education by metaphor. We insist that this is certainly the only sound religious education. As Mary sat absorbed at the Lord's feet, so are we to contemplate the great myths that constitute our richest heritage in the realm of the Spirit, to try "all" in imagination, and to hold fast to those which seem to us most faithfully to illuminate our world and ourselves. But may we never forget that these are *myths* and therefore graciously allow the Unnamable to remain finally unnamed.

Chapter II

The Meaning of Mysticism

Having tried to define what I mean by religion, I now seek to delineate the peculiar approach to religious experience that has historically borne the name of mysticism. If religion is basically a quest for unity within and for harmonious relatedness to one's total environment, in the context of the best one can envisage, then mysticism will be seen as the way *par excellence* in which this quest is pursued.

I have concluded that it is well to retain the name "God" as the symbol of that ultimate reality to which religion addresses itself. So I find it necessary to retain the word "mysticism" for that form of experience which I must now attempt to describe. Apart from the word "God" and perhaps the word "religion" itself, no other word has been more abused in the history of religion. Some writers have undertaken to coin some new word or phrase. Much as I should like to disabuse this word of the misconceptions that have clung to it, the experience to which I shall point has been called by this name so long that we shall do ourselves a great disservice to abandon it now. We need to understand the development of the experience in history, its variations, even its aberrations, if we are to free it for continued service as a symbol of central significance. I shall attempt to invest it with peculiar meaning and fresh significance for our own day without severing it from its historical roots. This book is an "apology" for mysticism in the classic theological sense of interpretation and defense. Despite those unfortunate accretions, which have sullied the term, it is my purpose once more to exalt it.

In her book *The Meaning and Value of Mysticism,* Emily Herman begins her introductory statement with an eloquent appraisal of "the perennial philosophy," as it has served the Christian religion.

> Beneath the currents which by action and reaction have gone to shape Christian thought there sounds, like the fabled sunken bell, the strain of Mysticism. Thrust down by victorious institutional, rational and moralistic forces, the mystic note floats up from the depths—now muffled, now clear. Every now and again the penalty of success overtakes the ruling system, and Christian men, disillusioned by hollow civilisation and an externalized Church, listen to the submerged melody and find it a song of deliverance; and out of such moments of reaction are born the great spiritual movements, whether explicitly mystical or only showing deep affinities with Mysticism.[4]

WHAT MYSTICISM IS NOT

In my attempt to describe mysticism, I shall refer to mystical experience rather than to mystical philosophy or mystical theology which have emerged in reflection upon the experience. Let me begin by eliminating those forms of experience which we must disallow as representing genuine mysticism. Just as in the Orient some undertook the designation of God by the dialectic process, *neti, neti* ("not this, not that"), so it seems appropriate to begin by referring to those forms of experience with which mysticism has sometimes been confused.

Some distinguished scholars in the first half of the twentieth century gave themselves to research in the field of mysticism. Baron von Hügel, Evelyn Underhill, Dean Inge, Emily Herman, Rudolf Otto, Rufus Jones, and Walter Stace are among the most distinguished. With the exception of Baron von Hügel's considerable influence upon Evelyn Underhill, these students worked in complete independence of one another. All of them sought to discover what might be called the essence of the mystical experience. The degree of their concurrence was quite extraordinary. At no place was it more significant than in their identification of types of experience that do not qualify as mystical.

All agreed that the mystical experience has no inherent relationship to fascination by or preoccupation with the occult, the esoteric, or any of the various forms of mystery-mongering or mystification with which it has been so often associated. It has nothing to do with spiritualism, with table turning, with clairvoyance, or with any of the common forms of extrasensory perception. It is perfectly true, as these observers of the historic phenomenon have acknowledged, that a number of individuals who have had acceptable mystical experiences have also had psychical experiences of these other kinds. Some have exhibited an interest in the occult or the esoteric. But I must point out that a number of the greatest mystics record none of these experiences, nor did they betray the slightest fascination with them.

In the second place, we must dissociate from the essence of mysticism all forms of audible or visual experience. Once again, a number of the mystics have heard voices or seen visions, and in some cases it would appear that an insight of considerable importance was imparted to them in this way. One thinks of the vision of Peter in the New Testament (Acts 10:9–16) and the way in which he was freed by it from a compulsive attachment to a ritualistic practice of abstinence from meat eating. One thinks also of Paul's experience on the road to Damascus (Acts 9:3–7) and of the voice that spoke to George Fox of Jesus. Still the greatest of the mystics, as judged by criteria I shall presently develop, even though some of them experienced visions or heard voices, distrusted these. They exercised considerable discipline in scrutinizing them to ascertain whether they contained anything valid by way of a message. It was because of the persistent association between experiences of this kind and mysticism that the distinguished church historian, Adolf Harnack, came to identify mysticism with "Catholic piety," an unfortunate fixation for a scholar otherwise distinguished for his critical acumen.

We must also separate in our thinking fascination by what purports to be supernatural suspension of physical law from having anything to do with mystical experience. Hence we shall have to distinguish between qualifications for the canonization of saints by the Roman Catholic Church and those by which we can recognize the developed mystic. To qualify as a recognized mystic within the Christian tradition, there would be no need for miracles if miracles mean the apparent supernatural suspension of physical law. Indeed, the greatest of the mystics have insisted upon an unbroken continuity between the natural and the supernatural, if indeed they use this latter term at all. For them it is always one world, not two. The supernatural has been understood by them to be the "natural," of which our present sensory-intellectual consciousness is not yet fully aware. Indeed, the only "miracle" that one thinks of in connection with these mystics is that characteristic transformation of their own persons. That transfiguration in the direction of interior unity and wholeness and characteristic "at-homeness" in their environment released them to become peculiarly effective human beings in their own spheres of endeavor. This basic miracle did sometimes enable them to exercise extraordinary influence upon others, whose potential unity they were thus enabled to elicit and draw forth by reason of loving identification. Freud said that all psychotherapy depends upon the crucial process of transference. The unforced identification of which the mystic is capable makes possible a relationship in which transference flows quite naturally. Moreover, the mystic, who is consciously centered in God, is often more able than the analyst to release the person from bondage to the transference because he or she interprets the object of the transference to be the God who dwells within this other as well as in the self.

That there should have been associations historically with the esoteric and occult is quite natural. The Greek word from which we derive our word "mystic" came out of the Greek mystery religions. The mystic was thought of as an initiate into the secret knowledge of divine things. Later the Neoplatonists developed a discipline intent upon deliberately closing one's eyes and other senses to all external things. This practice has had its counterpart in Eastern mysticism. It was only with the Reformation that the word was freed, at least for some, from these earlier references and came to be used for that form of experience which I shall now attempt to interpret.

MYSTICISM AS A NEW FORM OF CONSCIOUSNESS

It is always more difficult to describe what mysticism is than what it is not. Here one ought to recall the ancient counsel: "If one says what it is, he does not know, and if he knows, he does not say." As I write this, I remember an image of one of those strangely idealized countenances, drawn by Kahlil Gibran, with a finger upon its lips, sealing them against the impertinence of distraction by speech. Whatever one says represents in some sense a loss of power, a distortion, a betrayal, even a profanity. The mystics unanimously proclaimed that what they experienced was quite "ineffable." And yet, paradoxically, without exception they felt compelled to attempt to describe it; and they were at pains to fit it into a theological pattern or world view in which they were already at home. Hence we shall not break company with them if we are here constrained to point as best we may to so significant a reality.

The researchers to whom I have referred have thought of the mystical experience basically as reflecting a new form of consciousness. Dean Inge, for example, thinks of it as "an extension of the frontier of consciousness." He tells us:

> Mysticism arises when we try to bring this higher consciousness into relation with the other contents of our minds. Religious Mysticism may be defined as the attempt to realize the presence of the living God in the soul and in nature, or, more generally, as *the attempt to realize, in thought and feeling, the immanence of the temporal in the eternal, and of the eternal in the temporal.*[5]

Evelyn Underhill puts it this way:

> I understand it to be the expression of the innate tendency of the human spirit towards complete harmony with the transcendental order; whatever be the theological formula under which that order is understood. This tendency, in great mystics, gradually captures the whole field of consciousness; it dominates their life and, in the experience called "mystic union," attains its end. Whether that end be called the God of Christianity, the World-soul of Pantheism, the Absolute of Philosophy, the desire to attain it and the movement

towards it—so long as this is a genuine life process and not an intellectual speculation—is the proper subject of mysticism. I believe this movement to represent the true line of development of the highest form of human consciousness.[6]

Walter Stace, in his *Teachings of the Mystics,* attempts to take as his distinguishing norm for it the words in the Mandukya Upanishad, one of the earliest and most profound of mystical treatises:

> Beyond the senses, beyond the understanding, beyond all expression . . . it is the pure unitary consciousness, wherein awareness of the world and of multiplicity is completely obliterated. It is ineffable peace. It is the supreme good. It is one without a second. It is the Self.[7]

This latter is, I think, a description of a particular form of mysticism carried to its logical conclusion within the context of Eastern philosophy. I would not want so narrowly to define the consciousness of which we are speaking, certainly not within the Christian context. There is a distinguishing characteristic about this form of consciousness that might be called "unitary" since it tends to perceive relatedness. But it is certainly not true that an awareness of the world or even of multiplicity is necessarily "obliterated." It would be more accurate to say that the many are perceived as within, or in some sense related to each other in, the One.

We insist with Dean Inge that there is no faculty above reason, "if reason is used in its proper sense as the logic of the whole personality." He properly amended a statement by Harnack to the effect that "mysticism is nothing else than rationalism applied to a sphere above reason" by insisting that what Harnack ought to have said was: "Mysticism is nothing else than reason applied to a sphere above rationalism." [8]

We recognize a truth in Goethe's famous definition: mysticism is "the scholastic of the heart, the dialectic of feelings." But any attempt to separate the various functions of the personality into will, emotion, and reason, as if these could operate separately, inevitably leads to an artificial construction of the human psyche. The mystical sense, according to Emily Herman, is in reality nothing else than the intellectual, volitional, and emotional powers turned upon their source and goal. . . . It is not something moving the reason, directing the will, setting the emotion on fire; it is reason, will, and feeling exercising their most truly natural function—the whole personality of man in contact with its source and end.[9]

We need in our day to put this whole question of the mystical experience as a form of consciousness into the perspective of the evolutionary process itself. As Teilhard de Chardin has shown clearly in his book *The Phenomenon of Man,* there has been an unbroken continuity in the evolution of this planet and of life upon it. The succession has been from molecular substance to cellular substance under certain conditions that obtained during one apparently unrepeatable period in the past. Since then, from cellular substance to ever more complex organisms, until at last reflective mind emerged in man. As Julian Huxley has pointed out, evolution became conscious of itself in man. And out of the reflective mind, which is a form of higher consciousness, spirit at length arose. Since one of the criteria of advance in the evolutionary process has been the expanding consciousness in the animal in terms of awareness of environment, until the animal, man, could even perceive values of a nonsensory kind, quite naturally we look for continuing evolution in man to produce yet higher forms of consciousness.

It is not surprising that we should look for this growing edge of the unfinished creation in humankind to take the form of an awareness or consciousness of aspects of reality which have not always been apparent to our forebears. Though everyone has this innate capacity in some degree, some individuals would have it more highly cultivated than others. We should expect it to be something which by usage, attention, and concentration could be further developed. I am making what may seem a presumptuous suggestion: mystical consciousness is that human faculty, new in evolutionary perspective, in which we can actually perceive the as yet unfinished creation still at work. Just as life emerged from matter, thought from life, spirit from thought, so mystical awareness now emerges from spirit. To put it another way, consciousness has come up out of the unconscious, and successively higher forms of consciousness continue to arise out of lower forms. The evolutionary process itself is characterized by "consciousness-raising."

I want to insist again that the mystical consciousness is not something with which only a few are endowed; it is found in everyone. All are special kinds of mystics, at least potentially. Some appear to be endowed with a greater capacity, and some, by disciplined effort, cultivate more fully what they have. We may look upon it as the one faculty that most awaits development if man is to realize his human potential and achieve a closer approximation to the society of which he dreams. Lecomte du Noüy in *Human Destiny* pointed out that, if our scale of observation be evolution rather than history, we can perceive greater importance in one person's loyalty to conscience than in all the political, social, and economic revolutions of our time. Similarly, we should attach evolutionary significance to the appearance and cultivation of the mystical capacity. Indeed, it is the mystical experience in one of its characteristic forms that produces and sustains conscience of a higher order.

What, then, does this form of consciousness perceive? It perceives unity, relatedness, wholeness. Walter Stace distinguishes between two forms of mysticism, the extroverted and the introverted. This distinction, it seems to me, is useful so long as we do not press it too far. He suggests that in the extroverted type the mystic perceives the characteristic undifferentiated unity through the senses. Within this category would come the nature mystics, many artists, and all those individuals who have felt themselves a part of a larger whole. Wordsworth speaks in his "Lines Composed Above Tintern Abbey" of

> . . . a sense sublime
> Of something far more deeply interfused,
> Whose dwelling is the light of setting suns,
> And the round ocean and the living air,
> And the blue sky, and in the mind of man;
> A motion and a spirit, that impels
> All thinking things, all objects of all thought,
> And rolls through all things.

The painter sometimes suggests in the form of his art the unity he perceives. In some of the paintings of Van Gogh, while the trees and grass remain distinctly trees and grass, they are clearly engaged in a common dance. Other artists have represented the same experience by reducing every stroke to a single dot in order to suggest that all the separate objects are reducible at last to a common element which binds them in some pattern of wholeness. A person of highly developed mystical capacity, like C. G. Jung, may have the experience of not knowing quite where his own body ends and an adjacent object begins. Jung describes in his autobiography, *Memories, Dreams, Reflections,* how, as a very young man, he was not sure of the distinction between himself and the stone upon which he sat. More common is that meeting in depth with another individual in which one experiences such a measure of unity that he is not quite aware to what extent he is living in that other or the other in him. All profound love between persons has some of this element in it.

On the other hand, the mystic of the introverted type looks inward and experiences at the depth of his being this unity with ultimate reality. The Buddhists have expressed it as that point at which the self and the Self are known to be one. A Christian might speak of that of God within or of that strange and paradoxical experience described by Paul as "I, yet not I, but Christ in me." Plotinus tells us that during the mystical experience the One appears:

> With nothing between . . . and they are no more two but one; and the soul is no more conscious of the body or of the mind, but knows that she has what she has desired, that she is where no deception can come, and that she would not exchange her bliss for all the heaven of heavens.[10]

MYSTICISM AS THE GROUND OF TRUE MORALITY

Within the mystical experience we find the deepest motivation for moral decision as well as the sharpest insight into the moral imperative. If the mystic actually experiences at some depth of his or her own being an inseparable oneness with the Absolute, that is the basis for the most profound self-love or self-reverence. One knows by direct experience that God himself is somehow present in the mystery of one's own identity and unique individuality. Whatever one's awareness of the depth of evil or potential for evil within oneself (and all the great mystics have been intensely conscious of this), there is no need to despair, to think of oneself as a worm, or as being utterly beyond the pale. As a human being, one is as capable of committing an unforgivable sin as God is of sinning against himself. Herein lies the good news which all the great mystics proclaim.

Because of this experienced unity between themselves and God, people can afford to be magnanimous toward themselves. They can afford to have sustained faith in their own capacity. They are able to exercise compassion toward themselves for their failures. But they will also have a poignant sense of the infinite pathos of their ever repeated "falls" and failures in relation to their aspirations. All people are at once far better and far worse than those nearest to them ever dream. To that degree in which we have cultivated the mystical faculty we affirm with Leon Bloy: "There is only one sorrow: not to be a saint." It seems to me a curious failure of insight when Auden insists, in his introduction to Hammarskjöld's *Markings,* that the author of those remarkable meditations had been mistaken in affirming that they contained the only true portrait of himself. It is Hammarskjöld whose instinct is unfailing here. We know the most important things about ourselves—if we are at all introspective, better than anyone else is able to divine. Others are more aware of our foibles, but of our "meanings," our aspirations, and longings, we are not only the better but the only judges, humanly speaking.

Observe, further, that the mystical capacity also enables a person to make the projection that on the interior stage of another human being's consciousness the same drama is taking place. One imputes to that other the same infinite pathos of striving to become fully human. Even if one is not aware of the peculiar aspirations of another, one yet knows that they are there. This is in part what makes one aware that both are bound into the same ground of being. In some profound sense one cannot be free while another is in fetters, nor rejoice while another suffers. Though Martin Buber in some of his writings disclaims mysticism, he was in reality, I believe, one of the great mystics of this century. Not only did he perceive the word of God in the event, "here where one stands," but he found the locus of the divine message in the "in-betweenness" of two people who come together in an I-Thou relationship. It is as if in such an encounter two persons perceived in this in-betweenness a reflection of the reality by which they are both sustained, and in which in some profound sense they are one. Before, above, and beyond the experience of "otherness" is an experience of likeness. The I and the Thou remain in dialogue, but the context in which the dialogue takes place is an undifferentiated unity which embraces both.

Observe another moral corollary. Since what binds two individuals together is that at the base of their separate identity there is God, taking another's life becomes impossible for one who experiences this insight. This is, I think, the reason why there has always been an affinity between the mystical consciousness and the acceptance of nonviolence as a way of life. Where mysticism has been strong, nonviolence has been practiced. To kill another becomes, within the context of the experience we have been describing, an act of deicide. Capital punishment also is seen to be a form of deicide, and participation in the killing in war involves both killing that of God in another person and that part of oneself which indwells another. That is to say, deicide, homicide, and suicide are all involved. This experience of mystical identification with others is the strongest motivation for morality. One is constrained to follow Kant's moral imperative, recognizing as just in one's own behavior only what one is prepared to universalize for all. Written upon the inward parts of the heart is the law, "Do unto others as you would that they should do unto you."

Walter Stace and others have observed that mystics need not be "religious" persons. That is, they may stand outside of any religious tradition, may even proclaim themselves atheists. But by our definition of religion they are as profoundly religious as any who stand within institutional religion. What is paramount in their experience is the same compulsion toward interior integrity and ever more creatively harmonious relationship with the total environment. They are, in effect, obedient to the religious impulse.

THE MYSTIC'S SELF-IMPOSED DISCIPLINE

The mystical consciousness comes initially as a free gift. Though there have been Yoga practices which purport to yield this blessing, and disciplines of prayer which, their advocates assure us, will produce this effect, most students of the subject and all the mystics themselves acknowledge that initially the experience comes as a divine gift. One does not take heaven by storm. Neither is it possible for this experience to come to one in the state of active violation of the moral imperative. What becomes immediately apparent to all who have bona fide mystical experiences, even of an elementary kind, is the painful disparity between their surface lives and that state of union which is experienced at a deeper level within them. Moreover, insofar as this experience takes the form of identification with others, the person becomes intensely aware of wrongdoing in his own patterns of behavior. When someone once put the question to Martin Buber, "What is sin?" he replied that he knew instantly in relation to himself, but hadn't the slightest idea what was involved in relation to any other person.

Since the experience has already carried its own interior assurance of unity with God and with one's fellows at some depth, the response to this appalling disparity between one's real self and one's surface behavior takes the shape not of remorse, which would be barren, but of repentance, which can be fruitful. In this experience of repentance is indicated the first step of the discipline known to all the major Christian mystics as purgation. What is amiss must be set aright. All that stands in the way of realizing in practice the demands of the interior vision, revealed as potential, must be abandoned. The person who has had a genuine mystical experience is motivated toward undertaking the path of renunciation.

The second stage has usually been called proficiency or illumination. After sustained practice of purgation, there comes
greater freedom, a new sense of wholeness and of growth. It is
not that purgation ever ceases, but that virtue can be gradually
practiced for its own sake, without the accompanying rigors and
the sense of being torn to pieces. There is not the same intensity
of the "war within one's members" that was earlier experienced.
There will still be times of lapsing. The "fall" is an ever repeated
act of existential failure. Yet there is an interior assurance, after
a time, which enables one to move forward in the life of the
Spirit.

The final stage is one devoutly to be wished; yet who shall
say it has in individual cases ever been attained in any sustained
way, save perhaps in Jesus of Nazareth. It has been called the
unitive life. This is in theory an unimpeded practice of the
presence of God. For those who do not think of themselves as
theists, it is a steady relatedness to the One, the Absolute, the
Ultimate Reality.

Though there are mystics who have pursued the appointed
disciplines in the hope of salvation, those with the greatest
insight have recognized that to seek God for any other purpose
than for union with him alone is to betray the vision. The
mystical consciousness is its own reward. At its best, it is not
a means to an end but is the end itself. It is realization, in the
New Testament sense, of the Kingdom of God within. It is
therefore a form of realized "eschatology," the Kingdom having
been attained, at least momentarily.

We must recognize an important difference between certain
forms of mysticism in the East and the best in the Western
tradition. In much of Eastern mysticism there has been the
unhappy notion that both matter and history are something to
be abandoned. The greatest heaven would be escape from the
cycle of reincarnation, a return to nothingness, a complete loss
of identity. Insofar as the way requires surrender of desire for
selfish ends of any kind it has its inevitable parallel in the West.
But when sensual imagery of all kinds, as well as intellectual
imagery, is thought of as evil or illusionary, and one attempts
to separate oneself wholly from the world, there enters a life

negation which is wholly in contrast with Christian mysticism at its best. There are some points of similarity as well. One of the greatest mystics, Meister Eckhart, can refer to the void, emptiness, etc. John of the Cross can speak of the dark night of the soul. There is paradox present, but the positive note of union with that which is real and which has its home in this world as well is never abandoned.

This basic distinction between some forms of Eastern mysticism and the classic forms in the West undoubtedly accounts for the failure in the East to produce a social consciousness and a capacity for involvement in history such as the West has known. At the same time, when the Buddha had achieved Nirvana, he paradoxically turned his back upon accepting it in order that he might convey the good news that would release his brethren from bondage. Moreover, many of the greatest Eastern mystics have a positive element of world affirmation, and posit no dichotomy between matter and spirit. On the other hand, in the later Neoplatonic tradition which passed almost entire into Christianity, there is much of the negative tendency. Therefore we must be wary of false generalization. There has been mysticism of a life-negating character in the West just as there have been strong currents of life affirmation in Eastern mysticism. Wherever the life-negating form has prevailed, moral distinctions have been lost, compassion has waned, and social concern has languished.

We have already admitted that there have been a number of unfortunate aberrations associated historically with mysticism. Later we shall deal in some detail with these. It is indeed a dangerous path. But there have always been dangers inherent in any advance in evolution. Many persons have lost their way, or wandered into a wilderness, pursuing a will-o'-the-wisp which ever eluded them. Nevertheless, at its best, mysticism would appear to point the way to a heightened sense of life, to a deeper involvement and commitment to it, and to the realization both of maximum individuation and at the same time a paradoxical sense of union with the eternal. In our day when our attention is likely to be drawn to feats of courage and adventure in outer space, the mystics

summon us to an inward journey. It is not an altogether un-
charted course. Many have groped their way through the
labyrinth within and have found at the core of their being
that they were awaited by One who made himself known to
them. Thereafter the world never appeared the same again.
Nor could they look again upon their fellows without concern. As Walter Stace puts it:

> The Christian mystics especially have always emphasized that mys-
> tical union with God brings with it an intense and burning love of
> God which must needs overflow into the world in the form of love
> for our fellow-men; and that this must show itself in deeds of char-
> ity, mercy, and self-sacrifice, and not merely in words.
>
> Some mystics have gone beyond this and have insisted that the
> mystical consciousness is the secret fountain of all love, human as
> well as divine; and that since love in the end is the only source of
> true moral activity, therefore mysticism is the source from which
> ethical values ultimately flow. For all selfishness and cruelty and evil
> result from the separateness of one human being from another. This
> separateness of individuals breeds egoism and the war of all against
> all. But in the mystical consciousness all distinctions disappear and
> therefore the distinction between "I" and "you" and "he" and
> "she." This is the mystical and metaphysical basis of love, namely
> the realization that my brother and I are one, and that therefore his
> sufferings are my sufferings and his happiness is my happiness. This
> reveals itself dimly in the psychological phenomenon of sympathy
> and more positively in actual love. For one who had no touch of the
> mystical vision all men would be islands. And in the end it is because
> of mysticism that it is possible to say that "no man is an island" and
> that on the contrary every man is "a part of the main."[11]

Now, finally, how does one know when an experience that
appears to be mystical is genuine? Rufus Jones provided us two
criteria of judgment which seem to me to be incontrovertible:
(a) there will be a marked increase in the coherence of the
personality; *(b)* there will be a heightened and sustained psychic
energy which will enable the person to carry out every ordinary
activity more effectively and with less fatigue.

WITNESS: THREE TWENTIETH-CENTURY MYSTICS

I call as witness three of the great men of our century: one a Protestant, one a Jew, and one a Roman Catholic. In each instance, behind the extraordinary integrity of the personality and the prodigious achievement in his field of labor, there lay, I am persuaded, a mystical experience. The experience came unsought and overtook the individual quite by surprise. Yet everything thereafter related in some sense to it. A sense of direction, of clarity, of vocation, and enough motivational fuel for a lifetime were provided. These three men are now dead.

The Protestant among our witnesses is Albert Schweitzer. His experience, recorded in his autobiography, is perhaps familiar to most of us:

> Slowly we crept upstream, laboriously feeling—it was the dry season—for the channels between the sandbanks. Lost in thought I sat on the deck of the barge, struggling to find the elemental and universal conception of the ethical which I had not discovered in any philosophy. Sheet after sheet I covered with disconnected sentences, merely to keep myself concentrated on the problem. Late on the third day . . . at sunset . . . there flashed upon my mind, unforeseen and unsought, the phrase, "Reverence for Life." The iron door had yielded: the path in the thicket had become visible. Now I had found my way to the idea in which world- and life-affirmation and ethics are contained side by side! Now I knew that the world-view of ethical world- and life-affirmation, together with its ideals of civilization, is founded in thought.[12]

The Jew is Martin Buber. It seems to me that it is not forcing the facts to suggest that his entire philosophy of dialogue, from which so much of his work derives and which has influenced Christian theology perhaps more than the work of any other theologian in this century, may well have its fountainhead in a mystical experience. He carefully buries it in one of his books, *Between Man and Man,* and relates it as if it had happened to another:

Imagine two men sitting beside one another in any one of the solitudes of the world. They do not speak with one another, they do not look at one another, not once having turned to one another. They are not in one another's confidence, the one knows nothing of the other's career; early that morning they got to know one another in the course of their travels. In this moment neither is thinking of the other; we do not need to know what their thoughts are. The one is sitting in the common seat obviously after his usual manner, calm, hospitably disposed to everything that may come. His being seems to say it is too little to be ready, one must be really there. The other, whose attitude does not betray him, is a man who holds himself in reserve, withholds himself. But if we know about him we know that a childhood's spell is laid on him, that his withholding of himself is something other than an attitude; behind all attitudes is entrenched the impenetrable inability to communicate himself. And now—let us imagine that this is one of the hours which succeed in bursting asunder the seven iron bands about our heart—imperceptibly the spell is lifted. But even now the man does not speak a word, does not stir a finger. Yet he does something. The lifting of the spell has happened to him—no matter from where—without his doing. But this is what he does now: he releases in himself a reserve over which only he himself has power. Unreservedly communication streams from him, and the silence bears it to his neighbor. Indeed it was intended for him, and he receives it unreservedly as he receives all genuine destiny that meets him. He will be able to tell no one, not even himself, what he has experienced. What does he now "know" of the other? No more knowing is needed. For where unreserve has ruled, even wordlessly, between men, the word of dialogue has happened sacramentally.[13]

The Roman Catholic is Pierre Teilhard de Chardin. Apparently his experience was not limited to one time and place but was one that grew throughout his life. Yet the initial and characteristic quality of it must have begun while he was quite a young man:

Throughout my life, through my life, the world has little by little caught fire in my sight until, aflame all around me, it has become almost completely luminous from within. . . . Such has been my experience in contact with the earth—the diaphany of the divine at the heart of the universe on fire. . . . Christ; His heart; a fire: capable of penetrating everywhere and, gradually, spreading everywhere.[14]

Chapter III

The Cultivation of the Mystical Faculty

If mysticism is the growing edge of man's evolving consciousness, then the cultivation of this faculty should become a major concern in religious education. It affects the education of our children as well as our own growth in the life of the Spirit as adults. We shall address this chapter to considerations relating to the implementation of this concern.

IMPLICATIONS FOR RELIGIOUS EDUCATION

Imparting the Idea of God Within

Let us first see what this would mean in planning the religious education of a child. Our major objectives would be: to enable a child to grow into an awareness of the divine spark within, to experience a lively sense of relatedness to his or her environment, and to identify with other creatures, particularly other human beings: As it is, there is an unconscious conspiracy on the part of adults to impose upon the child from the very beginning a sense of separateness. A boy, for example, is given a name and is told where his room is. He has his own toys. Everything speaks of distinctions. Very little tells him that he is bound into a common ground of being with everything and everyone else. The process of individuation will be lifelong, and is indeed "the quest of the holy grail," as Jung called it. But it must be pursued within the context of the mystery of oneness.

The first thing that must be said is that religion, especially this kind of mystical religion, is largely caught rather than taught. To be exposed to the kind of adult who has the authentic qualities of inwardness and gatheredness, developed through prayer and contemplation, is the best fortune that can befall the child. He will then imbibe in the most natural way the attitudes that will dispose him toward such development of the mystical faculty as may be further encouraged in other ways. Hence the first requisite for adults, if they would influence the child's basic religious growth, would be to seek growth themselves in the life of the Spirit through those disciplines we shall presently describe.

There are, however, certain insights that can guide the adult in planning the kinds of experiences and exposures that would be consonant with the inward development we have in mind for this child. We must confess quite frankly that just as no one can take by storm the heaven of mystical experience, so no one can produce or elicit such an experience in another. As Thomas Merton recognized, even a father cannot have this experience for his own son. There is always a "givenness," a completely unplanned and unsought quality about every genuine mystical experience. At the same time, there are certain inward postures of the Spirit and practiced ways of relating to one's total environment and to other human beings that quite clearly keep the windows open. There are others which seem rather effectively to keep them closed.

I suggest that this hypothetical child, whom we shall educate, be thought of as your "God-child." You are appointed to perceive and to relate to that of God in him, assuming it is a boy. This would mean, at the very least, that you would impart to him a sense of his own very great worth, furthering a positive self-image. In doing this you would be doing something much more important. You would be imparting to him the first faint glimmering that the fleeting beauty you perceived in him was not solely his. Something that dwelt within him and in some mysterious way shone through him was at once part of the very essence of his own identity as a person. At the same time it was the very point at which he was bound into a ground of being with all others. It was at once his self and the Self, his unique individuality and that which he could also find in others, if he but knew the secret of how to look.

You are smiling now at the presumption that so subtle an idea can be imparted to a child. But I am maintaining that he can indeed gradually apprehend this idea, on the unconscious level at least, from his observation that you relate to other children and to other adults as if they too had something of infinite value in them. This endlessly fascinating and enchanting search for God in his children becomes an unspoken secret that you share with this child. Meantime, the central insight of the mystic is taking root in this God-child of yours: the notion of immanence, God within his creation. Introducing this child to this quest for beauty is preparing him for the most profound lifelong joy. He need not then be later afflicted in mid-life by Augustine's poignant sorrow, alluded to in the Foreword: "O Beauty, so old and so new, too late have I loved thee!"

To use a crass phrase from our pragmatic vernacular, you will be conditioning this child in such a way as to make it just possible for him to respond to Teilhard's vision of "the diaphany of the divine at the heart of the universe on fire." The gift itself remains God's right of bestowal, not yours. You will only be precluding such conditioning as would make him nearly invulnerable to the shafts of God's wounding love. You counterbalance some of the defenses with which our heartless and technological age is all too ready to equip him. When at length he is old enough to assume mature responsibility as a neighbor, he will know intuitively that it is not good fences primarily that make good neighbors, that there is indeed something "that wants them down," and that this something that he might have named "elves" as a child "isn't elves exactly." He will little by little grow in that all but incommunicable inner preoccupation of perceiving strange likenesses between apparently disparate objects, a curious matrix or unity which somehow contains the multiplicity of things, a divine milieu which is at once the center or core and the environment, an elusive "in-betweenness" which arises whenever there is genuine dialogue between man and man.

What to Do About the Presence of Evil Within

At this point we must insert into our reflections a balancing insight. The primary emphasis is to be placed on the image of God in people, and the basic compatibility between matter and spirit, since matter in our experience is the only "conductor" for spirit. Nevertheless, there is in this world the terrible reality of evil. So long as the child very early learns the code for the language of religion, that it is always spoken in metaphors and parables, it will do him no harm to realize that, figuratively, there is also a generous proportion of "that of the devil" in him as well as in others. It is well to depersonalize it, and refer instead to the demonic. Experientially, however, he will sometimes feel "possessed" by something singularly like another being or something that transforms him into an apparently different "being." Unless you are a saint, or he is totally unobservant, he will know you as "possessed" on occasion too! This darkness or interior "shadow," if not of God, is yet permitted to exist by God. There must be no hint of dualism. God is one, the creator of good and evil alike.

The main thing is that the child be spared the false conviction that Augustine and Calvin elaborated with great ingenuity. That is the notion that a human being is by nature totally depraved, unless and until a God, quite exterior to him, rescues him and appoints him to the elect. Instead, there must be imparted to him that there is in the depths of his being an inviolable core of divinity, a sanctuary that nothing he has done or could do would finally desecrate. I believe there is clear evidence that this was Jesus' own view and that this was in fact the "good news" he preached.

The dynamic engagements of life, in which good and evil are clearly at war, will often obscure from the child's view the presence of this inner sanctuary. He may well despair from time to time of its existence, and look in vain for evidence of its presence in others. But the important thing is that when he resists evil, frees himself or is freed from possession by it, it is like "coming to himself" in Jesus' metaphor in the parable of the prodigal son. It is like coming home. This is quite different from imbibing from his earliest days the idea that his deepest and truest self, his real "me," is basically evil; that his only hope is a miraculous escape *from* himself, arranged by an absentee God who apparently plays favorites. Under no circumstances is he to be told that most cruel lie, which has produced more mental illness of a certain kind than any other: namely, that he or anyone else is capable of committing a permanently unforgivable sin.

How shall we account to the child for the presence of sin in the world and in himself? Certainly not by any mechanical notion of a "fall" by the first man, whose consequences we have inherited. From our evolutionary perspective there was no first man. Nor has there been in the past, whether one's scale of observation be evolution or history, any single sin or event which constituted a fall from which all persons now suffer. Sin is infinitely more "original" than that! It is indeed always original in that it takes the ever new and forever unrepeatable form of the unique individual's peculiar estrangement from himself, from his fellows, from his environment, and from God. Of its intensity only he and God can judge. It is to be measured, as he well suspects, by that distance between his conscious being at any moment and the purity of that temporarily untended inner sanctuary, the presence of which we hope we have been instrumental in making him aware. This is the place where his real self and God are inseparably one.

In a world created by a good God how did sin come into being? In a universe whose ultimate characteristic is grace, why is it so active? These are problems for which I believe there has never been a satisfactory solution. This is an unresolved paradox, hidden within the archetype of the self and of God. But this is not to say that we do not have insights into its nature. Sin is that which works against the texture of bondedness, wholeness, relatedness, integrity. It is what builds walls of separation. It is related to the hubris that wants to make one's own unruly desires the standard of values and therefore works estrangement within and without. We are sometimes beguiled by what Kierkegaard called "infinite possibility." Sin tends to produce a divided personality, whose parts are not integrated. Sin produces exactly the opposite of what we have defined earlier as the religious faculty. Instead of the motivation to bind things together in one bundle, it is the compulsion to separate things from each other, to compartmentalize the mind, and to enter into mutually contradictory human commitments.

There is about sin an inevitable aspect of self-betrayal, of "infidelity" to the self. If moving toward unity within is moving toward ever richer life and wholeness, sin is movement in the direction of disunity, ultimate dissociation. Growth in the life of the Spirit carries with it a sense of enhanced "being," involvement in sin a sense of increasing "non-being." When movement is in the direction of sin, the Self or God within is increasingly overlaid and obscured by surface, existential conflict. There is less and less relatedness between the Self and the self in given moments. A kind of living death ensues, which the Bible correctly assessed as the wages of sin. The Old Testament suggests that "the fear of the Lord is the beginning of wisdom." I am suggesting that we understand by the "Lord" here the law written upon our hearts. Loss of a sense of identity, through interior conflict and dismemberment, is indeed the hell of the "angst." It is the threat of non-being. To fear the "Lord" or the Law in the sense of respecting and obeying involves for us a life-and-death struggle to realize the never-to-be-repeated opportunity in this life to become and to remain our true selves.

Even a child can catch the first principle of this idea. When he is relating to himself, to his environment, and to others in a harmonious or potentially harmonious way, he has become himself, or is becoming himself. The "courage to be," as Tillich put it, is to be developed in him, and the movement in the direction of non-being to be deflected. When he has so moved, the wrong is to be acknowledged, not winked at. A way forward, a way home, a way to himself is to be indicated and facilitated through forgiveness, acceptance, and compassionate understanding. From your attitude he will learn how to forgive himself and to be compassionate toward himself in the presence of the pathos of the distance between his aspirations and his performance. Knowing that a like interior drama is taking place in others, he will exercise compassion toward them and remain nonjudgmental.

One other insight regarding sin needs to be conveyed to the child. Evil can constitute the very stuff out of which, by conversion of energy, good can come. We must embrace the ultimate paradox: God is the God of good and evil alike. His ways are past finding out. In the strange and unaccountable economy of the universe, not only do "all things work together for good to them that love God," but all things that have been in human experience, which are inevitably brought forward in memory, can be radically reworked for good when one begins to love the Lord. As distinct from that rare once-born soul identified by William James, for those of us who must be born over and over again this is the greatest good news of all. In the new texture of one's life these threads can be so rewoven as to constitute a part of the beauty of the new pattern. Even a child can be brought to see not only that he can in a real sense walk away from the wrong he does, from time to time, and return to himself, but also that he need not burden himself with the fear that he is destined to some future accounting for these sins, do what he will. God not only forgives. He even forgets. God forgets, because it is what one does with one's sin in the remaking of one's life that matters. And the "shadow" in the unconscious bears testimony of a neglected or unrecognized aspect of the self that needs to be integrated on the conscious level in order that true individuation or integrity may be realized.

How does the experience we are describing relate to the traditional experience of conversion, of being saved by Jesus the Christ? For my own part, I must distinguish between the Jesus of history and the Christ myth about him. The myth fused the messiah concept of Israel with the Hellenistic idea of the logos, or Word. It continues to project upon the historical figure all that has been imagined to be the nature of God. Many Christians still proclaim that Jesus was God or at least God's only Son. He entered the world and died upon the cross in order to save the human race. Now risen and sitting at the right hand of God he continues to save one by one those who will acknowledge him as Lord. Others of us may look back with considerable nostalgia upon a faith that has reoriented so many lives and produced such good works. Alas, we shall never again be able to embrace the ancient metaphor, in its earlier, literal sense, even by a leap of faith. Yet we can have the counterpart of the redemptive experience. There is a presence, God himself, to be known in the depths of our own being as the Christ or the Holy Spirit within, as well as in his transcendence, who accepts and forgives us because we are inseparably one with him. He would as readily reject himself as disown us.

Notice that in recognizing the presence of sin in ourselves we have pointed to the reality of the transcendence of God. This is a guarantee against the error of all forms of pantheism which undercut the basis of any distinction between good and evil. There is that of God in everyone. This is the first and great truth about ourselves. But there is also that of evil in us despite this implied and unexplained paradox with regard to creation by a good God who is also conceived as all-powerful. We are made in the image of God, but we are not God, as we well know whenever we "come to ourselves." God is immanent in his universe. This is why it is possible for a mystic like Teilhard to say, "Throughout my life, through my life, the world has little by little caught fire in my sight until, aflame all around me, it has become almost completely luminous from within." It has become luminous from within—precisely because the world is not itself the light! If the mystic saw God everywhere, indiscriminately, the mystic would see him nowhere. If everything were God, God were nothing. The authentic mystic's experience does not reflect pantheism, but rather panentheism, God in some sense in everything.

The mystic is of all people the most clear that, while there is that of God within, not all that is within is of God! Moreover, this presence of God within came from somewhere before this individual was, and inevitably points beyond itself to an existence, a measure of being and plenitude, infinitely beyond this miniscule representation. Far from denying transcendence, the experience of immanence is really the only thing that convincingly confirms it. Indeed the only clue as to the very existence

of the transcendent Christian God has been the experience of
him as immanent in people. Directly from his own interior
experience, the child can be taught, as he grows, to extrapolate
the transcendence of God.

THE MEANS OF RELIGIOUS EDUCATION

Learning the Language of Myth and Metaphor

We have suggested what some of the basic ideas are with
which you can help this God-child of yours toward self-under-
standing. The central idea is that there is that of God within,
the divine image, an infinitely precious presence, since it has
only this one chance of taking this peculiar expression within
this unique child. Now to make some more specific suggestions.
He must be encouraged to cultivate in a creative way his gift of
imagination. You will recall Robert Frost's assertion that all
sound education save that of mathematics is education by metaphor. This is especially true of religious education. This God-
child of yours is to be confided this great secret from the beginning, not awakened to it in dismay in mature years: all ways of
speaking of God are metaphors, *including* the doctrines of the
church.

We do not apologize for saying they are metaphors. Metaphors are not only the greatest symbols we have for reflecting
concepts of the nature of God, they are the only ones, aside from
their elaboration in what we call parables. If the child is encouraged to invent and to use metaphors and to respond to them in
great poetry and games of make-believe, it will be no shock to
him to discover gradually that the Christ myth is a metaphor
too, as is the very idea of an immanent-transcendent, personal
God. He will be taught how to distinguish between the Jesus of
history and the Christ metaphor for the reality of that Spirit
which lived in Jesus and can live in us in some indeterminate
measure. He will be introduced to other metaphors by which
other living religions have sought to point to the reality of the
divine in all persons, and to the projection of the idea of unlim-

ited divinity upon an imageless God, the central mystery of the universe.

Robert Hutchins, in evolving with others the idea of the Great Books Series, spoke of the essence of education as an exposure to greatness. Part of the religious education of your God-child will then be exposure both to the history of great ideas and to great persons, not only in the flesh but in great biography and autobiography. Committing to memory passages of poetic quality, especially from our own Scriptures, will be a valuable storage in the mind of metaphors which will help him to understand and to interpret to himself the hidden meaning of much of his own experience as it develops.

Cultivating Silence in Solitude

To learn how to sit quietly and to occupy the mind with reflection and to explore the beginnings of contemplation can be encouraged by participation in silent worship. Most children have much more natural aptitude for the practice of periods of silence than have adults. We are often overtaken in silence by the myriad voices of dangerous impulse, fantasy, and repression from the unconscious. A child appears to come "trailing clouds of glory" before "the weary weight of all this unintelligible world" hangs too heavily upon him. Moreover, a child can be encouraged to come to himself in creative silence as well as to experience a deeper closeness to others. Gradually he can learn the wisdom of the metaphor: "To hear the voice of the voiceless one must be silent before him" (Fénelon).

The natural posture for adoration is silence, while praise may speak or sing. One of the most important religious skills is just this capacity to adore. These fleeting glimpses of divinity perceived in oneself and in others, and in characters in literature —one must learn to draw toward them in loving identification, or at least in longing and aspiration! As the child must learn to distinguish between metaphor and reality, so must he distinguish between persons and that which he adores in them, lest he be hung up by any crippling fixations. Even more than her responsibility to wean him from the milk of her breasts, the mother has the grave responsibility to wean her child away from an adoration directed to her. Gently but firmly she must lead him to direct it toward the same trustworthy source of love and concern in other conveyors, especially toward that of God in himself.

A Knowledge of Evolution and of Ecology

We turn now to another important aspect of this God-child's proper religious education. Our unconscious conspiracy to make him feel separate from others makes more difficult his realization that he is one with all others. Just so, our urban civilization conceals from him the fact that his life is totally dependent upon the interrelatedness of the flora and fauna in the biosphere that encircles the globe. Therefore the study of paleontology or evolution should be prescribed as part of his religious education. Also the science of ecology is to be a required course for him at some early stage of his development. He is not only to have an academic knowledge of his enmeshment in the precious web of life, but, especially as a child, he must have opportunities to live close to the earth. He needs to experience the earth's bounty, its changing moods, its infinitely varied texture, and its diverse forms of hospitality to different creatures under varying circumstances. He can never develop a sense of the species to which he belongs, and of loyalty to it as above all loyalties to section, class, race, or nation, unless he "experiences," as well as thinks about, the interdependence of all living things on this planet, and their dependence in turn upon the elements themselves. It is not enough to feel that he belongs to his family, his friends, his neighborhood, his city, his nation. He must experience belonging to the species and to the good earth which has reared him. Poets like Wordsworth can tell him a little of what he has experienced or can experience. But he must roam the hills, the dales, the woods, alone, and sometimes with beloved companions. Conservation will then be a deep part of his commitment to the earth. In his love of nature he may even come to know a little better nature's God, catching glimpses of him "in the diaphany of the divine at the heart of a universe on

fire." He must learn to know existentially what the word "coin-
herence" signifies.

The mien of nature's countenance is not always friendly, but
the God-child will learn that nature is not willfully alien to him,
though he can be willfully alien to nature. Nature is indeed often
"red in tooth and claw," but not with that admixture of ugly
hatred of which the human mind is capable. He will not interpret nature's tragedies as "acts of God" but as part of the
interplay of that same "time and chance" which, as Ecclesiastes
observed, "happeneth to all." Hence he will be able to look with
equanimity upon nature's apparently wayward moods, knowing
that she yet supports him on her bosom. It is we rather than
nature that threatens, through atomic weapons, so to disturb her
delicate balance as to make whole sections of the earth uninhabi-
table. In one of the last articles that Aldous Huxley wrote before
his death, he reported that the time had come when the only
politics left with any remaining relevance is the "politics of
ecology." We can at least point our children to that day when
the science of ecology will indeed persuade humanity that the
only practical thing to do for the preservation of the species is
to convert our swords into plowshares and our spears into pruning hooks.

Along with this capacity to see himself within the biological
space-time continuum, you would want your God-child to feel
not only identified with the achievements and the joys of others
in the one human family but also involved in others' sufferings
and sorrows. Much as we might cringe from exposing him at a
tender age to the many dimensions of suffering in the world, we
do him greater disservice by attempting to protect him from
them. We make it harder for him to accept death by shielding
him too long from its stark reality. We need sensitivity in knowing how much the individual child can bear at a given time. But
unless he early experiences this kind of empathic identification
with human suffering, it will not readily come to him later on.
As we have been at pains to point out, this inward consciousness
of mystical identification is the strongest motivation for compassionate action. Henri Bergson insisted that of the two sources
of morality and religion—ritual and legalistic codification on

the one hand and mystical consciousness on the other—mystical consciousness is infinitely the more important and effective. What Paul was able to say out of his experience in relation to the brethren, you might aspire toward on behalf of your God-child, in relation to the whole human family:

"Who is weak, and I am not weak? Who is made to fall, and I am not indignant?" (II Cor. 11:29). What a "tendering" this would be. He need not then wait for dramatic forms of injustice to speak to his conscience, but will develop his own concerns, directly through the involvement of his own creative, empathic capacity for identification.

We must realize that there are a number of different psychological types. Jung's set of four is perhaps still useful: thinking, feeling, intuition, and sensation. The Hindus speak of four ways to God, adapted to four different kinds of people: through knowledge, through love, through work, and through psychological exercises or experiments. There are an infinity of combinations taking into account introversion and extroversion. These will determine the form the mystical experience will take if it comes. Some experience union with God primarily through the intellect, some through feeling, some in action, and some through intuition. But whatever the variation in the personality makeup of your God-child, there are certain constants in the exposures and disciplines we have recommended from which all could benefit.

THE ADULT'S QUEST FOR CONTINUED GROWTH

The best thing you can do for your God-child is to pursue faithfully your own quest for growth in the life of the Spirit. What shall we say then of the adult's cultivation of the mystical faculty? We must first observe that as adults we do not wholly outgrow the child's needs. These very opportunities we plan for our God-child must so order our own lives as to provide for our growth.

We will have discovered those occupations, those creative talents which work to the soul's health. Whether it be music, art, craft, we will have discovered what nourishes us, what frees us from the burden of self, what enables us to grow. We will have learned the optimum proportions of exercise, rest, dietary practices, that enable us to be at our best, though disciplined observance is a lifelong struggle. We will need to get back to the earth and the elements periodically, and to commune with land, sea, sky, flora and fauna.

Especially we will need to find those companions of the spirit, the developed mystics, who speak to our condition and to devote some time regularly, preferably daily, to unhurried, reflective, meditative reading of their writings. While response to the devotional classics is an individual matter, for the Christian the Bible is universal in its appeal because it is itself a whole library of devotional books. Therefore we will return ever and again to the Bible. It is interwoven with so much else in our Western culture that if we do not keep conversant with it, we cut ourselves off from an important segment of our roots. We will therefore fail to recognize instructive allusions to it that meet us everywhere. In these writings one sees oneself as in a mirror in ever new ways. We meet ourselves in the Bible under the aspect of eternity and in the presence of God.

What of the traditional practice of prayer that has always been considered the lifeblood of the church? When God is understood as a symbol for a reality that is not conceived as a person, what happens to prayer? As someone has expressed it, "How does one pray to a metaphor?" This is a real problem that must be faced honestly. Consider that no one has seen God at any time. His very existence is a conjecture and a projection from the human mind in the context of complete mystery and want of objective knowledge. We are therefore justified in concluding that the use of the metaphor or image of "person" for God is more satisfactory than the metaphor of law or principle or abstract concept.

We experience existentially that this reality we name God has attributes we can associate only with a person-like being. We impute to this reality the ultimate source and final meaning of these very attributes of love, tenderness, forgiveness, grace. These we experience initially in some measure in relationship to other human beings, else the very word symbols would have no meaning. But these person-related realities, as far as we know, have been released in the evolutionary process with the advent of man. We conjecture that they have a source beyond us and the possibility of an expression more whole and complete than the imperfect and fragmented form in which we encounter them in actual relations to other persons. Their author, sustainer, and "expressor" must be "personal," however much more he may —indeed, must—be. We are entitled at least to relate to this unknown reality as if he were person-like.

When we do so, when we deliberately will to react to this reality as to a Self, both within our selves and beyond, there are both intimations and assurances that a "Thou" responds. There is the strange impression that we are already in some sense "known" by this Thou; that he has already sought us before we sought him. We cannot know that there is a God and that he is a person in the sense in which we know the existence of objects through the senses. We must also be humble enough to admit that this reality we call God may be quite other than this meta-phor of person we use to present him. Yet the very disciplined relating to the Supreme Mystery in I-Thou categories produces a measure of health and wholeness not otherwise attainable. Since a dimension of life consonant with growth and develop-ment is added in this way, we are entitled to participate know-ingly in this living myth, to experiment further with this "model."

Hence, as adults we must impose upon ourselves a discipline in the life of prayer we cannot require of our God-child. None of the traditional kinds of prayer can be eliminated safely from our spiritual diet. It is important to practice adoration, for this is the process by which we become ever more like that to which we are drawn in a sustained way. Praise is properly a part of the practice of adoration. In proportion as adoration is vital, we will be "tendered" inwardly, kept alert and perceptive in relation to the Beauty, "so old and so new," that eludes all but those who train themselves to find some trace of it every day. It greets us unexpectedly in passersby on the city streets, whose momentary glance and smile betray the presence of the royal guest within. It rises to salute our inward eye from the printed page during our devotional reading, in an image, or in a drawing together of ideas, never before quite so felicitously wedded within our memory. It joins us as a silent presence in a place that custom has hallowed by corporate worship. It gently woos us in the fragrance of "a new smell," a homely phrase which George Fox used to describe a suddenly transformed earth. At other times, it is as if "new eyes for invisibles" had been bestowed, to borrow Rufus Jones's expression.

To the psalmist, it was a joyful and pleasant thing to give thanks. It would be a contradiction in terms to be at once somber and thankful. Those who recount their blessings one by one, in solitude every day, are not so likely to take any of them for granted, nor to assume that the world owes them a living. Thanksgiving is one form of prayer that cannot be performed from a sense of duty. To be authentic it ever springs in spontaneity. But this is not to say a time ought not to be reserved for its practice, a time not grudged but cherished and eagerly anticipated every twenty-four hours. To whom is the thanksgiving directed? To the mysterious source of life and bounty both within and without, to this Self within and, beyond our self, to God.

What will be our approach to confession as a form of prayer? I might make my confession to some trusted spiritual guide and receive by substitution from him the forgiveness of mankind. Fortunate the person who has such a confessor. All of us need one. But there are secret sins of impulse and imagination which we do not know how to confess to anyone. Once again we turn quietly to that God who is both creator and sustainer of the universe and the interior monitor: "ultimate demand and final succor." The existential sins of my ego self must be confessed to this unstained Self within. My alienation from this divine spark within is my primary problem, reconciliation my major responsibility. And this prayer of confession must never be concluded without the twofold inward movement of repentance, that is, turning away from the sin in imagination and will, and receiving joyously and freely the proffered forgiveness from the Self to myself.

For the aspiring mystic who is growing in a sense of unity

with God, intercession is quite transformed from its accustomed character. It is not forgone but is deepened and elevated. One no longer asks God for favors for one's friends. One is not less importunate than the widow, pounding at the door of the heartless judge, but the door is not closed and he who dwells within is not primarily a judge at all. In the lovely phrase of *The Book of Common Prayer,* not only is God already "doing for them better things" than one can "desire or pray for," but the only blessing one ought to plead for is a conscious nearness to God, whatever the accompanying suffering. Since that other for whom one makes intercession is bound into the same ground of being, keeping one's own channel open affords an additional access to the beloved for God. As for one's enemies, those individuals whom one cannot abide, here intercession takes two forms: the use of creative imagination in recollecting those qualities in the other which one can affirm before God, and the diligent search within one's self for the pride or fear that produces hostility and enables that other to constitute, in some sense, one's private hell. Sartre was wrong; there is an exit. It lies not in vain striving to transform that other, but in readiness to be transformed within, so that the other is secretly disarmed without any loss of face.

Petition for those who would cultivate the mystical life, selfish as it may seem, is one of the most crucial forms of prayer. This is because we well know the paradox that the very best we can do for others is to offer them our own best self. Petition is not the presumption of asking special gifts from God, material or spiritual. It is a persistent inward search for God. The open secret that all the great mystics have shared with us is that where God is to be found within, there the unique creature God intended is most likely to be. The Self of my self *is* God. The increasing petition is for God himself, not for anything he can give, though there remains place always for the childlike petition for oneself and all of humanity: "Give us this day our daily bread." In the daily inward search for God in one's self, and for one's self in God, the imperious demands are heard in terms of purgation: what physical or mental habit wants pruning or excision, that one may continue to grow in the life of the Spirit? The day's responsibilities are quietly reviewed before God. Opportunities are creatively met in imagination. "Whatever you ask in prayer, believe that you receive it, and you will." Here is that moment in prayer when one consciously receives "the courage to be," and evermore to become the self at the core of one's being.

We have spoken of the traditional forms of prayer reinterpreted and redirected by the mystical approach to religious experience. Now we must observe that petition, understood from this perspective, flows imperceptibly into the distinctive prayer of the mystics, variously called contemplation, adoration, the prayer of quiet, affective prayer. It involves a spirit of passive receptivity. From that depth of petition it is as if one overheard within one's self converse between the Father and the Son (to use P. T. Forsyth's description). One becomes still more attentive and focused. Here is the final "centering down," to use the still helpful metaphor dear to Friends. One awaits him who already awaits us at the center, while he abandons neither the infinite circumference of his universe nor his abiding place in eternity. Up to now one's prayer has been a sustained effort of reaching, aspiring, straining forward. Here one only waits in relaxed attentiveness and trust upon that ultimate character of the universe which reveals itself as grace. Here is the practice that produces what the mystics call illumination, the stage beyond purgation, yet always accompanied by demands for further purgation. The unitive life, attained intermittently perhaps by a few of the great mystics, and sustained to an extraordinary degree in Jesus, the Jewish mystic, is a pure gift from God. But one can do something to prepare to receive that gift, and on the way be prepared to endure dread and a deepening sense of the void and of nothingness.

The only way that one can hope to arrive at any measure of proficiency in the practice of the presence of God within and without is by faithfulness in the daily practice of devotional reading, meditation, and prayer. These disciplines will take specific forms as varied as the number who pursue them. But there are certain constants that we have recalled from the accumulated experience of the species in this central area of its most characteristic upreach and aspiration. These are to be experimented with in the solitude of each life, in the spirit that motivated Jesus: "For their sake I consecrate myself." For that hypothetical God-child, whom a mysterious providence has provided each one of us, we are required to consecrate ourselves by repairing inwardly to that secret place of the Most High where the Lord of Hosts already awaits our coming.

There is a great contemporary need for a marked increase in the number of competent guides in the "life of the Spirit," the life Paul described as "hid with Christ in God." The need has been recognized by Morton Kelsey, Douglas Steere, and many others. Simone Weil's assertion that nothing is so hard to find as a good confessor ("one may perchance find such once or twice in a lifetime") is still, unhappily, a valid observation. But new training centers are arising in response to the overwhelming need.

What is required, in my judgment, is a new creative wedding of the accumulated wisdom of the heritage of classic Christian spiritual direction and the new revelation concerning the nature of the psyche from the evolutionary and depth-psychological perspectives, especially those of Teilhard de Chardin and C. G. Jung. We must build on the phylum already in existence for centuries, but allow it to evolve and be updated and informed by new insights. This will inevitably involve, for guide and counselee alike, the cultivation of the mystical faculty.

Chapter IV

Vagaries and Aberrations of the Mystical Way

In advocating mysticism as the most mature form of religion, I have not denied that there are real dangers in pursuing this course. It is everywhere and always a narrow way that leads into life. We shall not expect to find it otherwise when the way is one that purports to lead into the richest and most rewarding life. If the destination is the peak of human experience, we shall not be surprised that the climb is precipitous and that fatal falls can be the consequence of missteps. The worst is always the corruption of the best, in religion as in every other human endeavor. The tragedy can be the greater here, however, because we are speaking, not of some optional avocation or tangential pursuit, but of what may spell the difference between personal salvation and damnation, whatever meaning we may wish to give these terms. Moreover, it is not merely a matter of life or death for the explorer, but may well affect profoundly the lives of others to whom he is intimately bound or upon whom he exerts influence.

PANTHEISM AND OTHER ATTEMPTS TO DEAL WITH THE PROBLEM OF EVIL

We have anticipated some of these dangers. Now we need to examine them with greater care. Orthodoxy in all the Western religions has always been wary of the heresy it has designated as pantheism, the complete identification of deity with everything that has been created. The concern has been well founded. Involved is the philosophical question: If God is equally everything, can he in fact be anything? There is also the moral issue: If he is equally manifest in every motivation and happening, can there be any valid distinction between good and evil?

The problem is infinitely heightened when it is transferred from intellectual theorizing to the context of mystical experience itself. If a man insists that he not only experiences a strange identification with objects of creation, trees, water, vapor, and all else besides but that he has discovered himself to be one with their creator and sustainer, what is to prevent him from concluding that he himself is above right and wrong? Or that he has assimilated unto himself the very attributes of God? Pantheism is bad enough when entertained as a theory. When it is fused with the interpretation of mystical experience, it has understandably been anathema, alike to Judaism, Islam, and Christianity.

It is little wonder that mysticism has been held suspect by the Western religions throughout their long history. Ecclesiastical authorities have intuitively recognized the besetting temptation that would appear to confront all mystics. We can understand how an experience of undifferentiated unity should be susceptible of a pantheistic interpretation. If I identify indiscriminately with everything in creation, I am likely to find it very difficult to find sufficient motivation to fight what Paul called the "good fight" against evil.

As long as the intellectual belief is entertained separately from involvement in relationship and vocation, the position may well be innocuous. But when one begins to act upon pantheistic conceptions, one's behavior inevitably takes on an amoral character. If God not only permeates the universe but *equally* coinheres all things, including all kinds of human institutions, and is coextensive with all that he has created, then one form of behavior cannot be commended above another. The root of moral earnestness is severed. From the point of view of theism this doctrine has always been unacceptable.

On the other hand, what has been called panentheism is acceptable. This is the doctrine that while God is the author of all things, he is not to be totally identified with what he has created. Like Teilhard, one may perceive the diaphany of the

divine in matter itself. But it does not follow that matter is itself
God. Else all matter would constitute an epiphany as well as
reveal a diaphany. Evil conduct and evil institutions may bear
witness to the reality of God in their very perversion of the good.
But evil is not therefore good. Nor are evil and good incarnate
forms of yin and yang, reflecting some eternal alternation like
the ebb and flow of the tides. Dante suggested that sin is mysteriously grounded in the good, and constitutes the perversion of
good. And Charles Williams held that "deep, deeper than we
believe, lie the roots of sin; it is in the good that they exist; it
is in the good that they thrive and send up sap and produce the
black fruit of hell."[15] But all attempts to account for the presence
of evil, however understood, in a universe created by a good
God are ultimately unsatisfactory, emotionally as well as intellectually. One must simply accept the ultimate paradox and
allow its mystery to remain unresolved.

The attempt of Christian Science to stare evil out of countenance has had a pragmatic value for certain types of personality.
But it has not and will not win widespread acceptance among
intellectuals. Jung's insistence that God himself be held responsible for the presence of evil has an appeal from the point of view
of logic and consistency in the inescapable monism that is characteristic of the mystic, but does not so far do justice to the
paradox that experience presents. The dualistic notion that two
gods, the god of evil and the god of good, are eternally at war
with each other is another attempt, variously presented, by some
of the historical religions to account rationally for the moral and
intellectual dilemmas that confront us. A variation of this approach, adapted to the modern evolutionary perspective, is that
of a good but limited God who is still evolving in a basically
neutral or amoral universe.

I believe that none of these attempts to make sense of the
nature of the universe as we know it can convince a questioning
mind or allay the demands of a passionate heart that has once
responded to the love of God. The mystic is inclined to accept
the paradox—the experience of God's goodness on the one hand
and his omnipotence and omnipresence on the other—without
striving to resolve it by an intellectual tour de force. In the end,

the mystic places a finger upon his lips in a plea for silence, not because he knows and will not share the intellectual answer to these riddles, but because he is prepared to let them continue to dwell in mystery and to trust, nevertheless, even unto the end. *Neti. Neti.* Not this. Not that. One may safely say what God is not, but who may presume to say precisely what God is?

THE DANGERS OF IDENTIFICATION WITH DEITY

By and large, the world has demonstrated a capacity to tolerate its pantheists, provided they do not attempt to undermine the reigning theoretical morality. Even the church, while adjudging the doctrine anathema, is not inclined to organize an inquisition against pantheists so long as they do not divert the faithful from the straight and narrow way.

What it has not been able to tolerate is another aberration of mystical experience in which the individual appears specifically to identify either with God himself or with the historical divine emissary on earth. This it designates blasphemy and reserves for it the most radical punishment. Had Jesus remained a rabbi and been able to convince the authorities that he was merely interpreting the law and the prophets and teaching a new life-style, he might well have been allowed to propagate his ideas. It was only when he claimed to be one with the Father, or accepted such appellations as Messiah and Son of God, that there were demands for his execution. When he seemed to claim to be the awaited Messiah, or did not disclaim the role when it was accorded him by his disciples, then began the relentless clamor to put him down.

When modern medicine began to study scientifically the phenomenon of psychotic identification with a divine figure, suspicion was thrown upon the sanity of the Jesus of history. Albert Schweitzer took it upon himself to produce a doctoral dissertation defending Jesus from the charge of paranoia.[16] He did so primarily on the ground that Jesus never exhibited the characteristic symptoms of withdrawal and of being out of touch with reality. On the contrary, in the vernacular of our time, he was invariably "with it," no matter what the circumstances and the pressures. Nevertheless, in the eyes of the contemporary hierarchy, he seemed to be accepting the role of Messiah, if not actually making himself equal with God. From our point of view, the innovation in his thought, namely, that the role of the Messiah involved the royal way of the holy cross, removed from him any guilt of hubris, much less blasphemy, even if he had accepted the appellation.

Meister Eckhart could preach his mystical theology with impunity as long as he spoke in abstract terms or indulged in allegory. But when he proclaimed "My me is God" he provoked the controversy that ended in his posthumous excommunication. Such statements can be symptoms of pathological hubris or paranoia. In Jungian terms, this would be an identification with an archetypal image, producing the psychological malady of inflation. With Eckhart, however, such statements must be interpreted in the context of his doctrine of the immanence of God and also of his way of life. There was nothing in his behavior that suggested psychosis or even that he thought more highly of himself than he ought to think. Nor was he making a claim that he would not have applied with equal passion to every other person in whom there had taken place what he chose to call "the noble birth in the life of the spirit."

It will be instructive, however, to see how, in a delicately balanced soul, a comparable claim, especially if it is taken up and pronounced in a literal sense by fanatical followers, may lead to disaster. Among the early Quakers none was more winsome or more effective in the ministry of the Word than James Naylor. We are told that he was as impressive in appearance as he was formidable as a disputant. An older colleague had admonished him with prophetic foresight "that thou steal not men's hearts away from God to thyself, and so lord it on their conscience that they have neither God nor scripture, nor any privilege of their own experience, but take thee as a demigod and to make thee a mental idol, which is a worse kind of idolatry than all that thee reproves."[17] Some women, described as having "much enthusiasm and little judgment," began to make extravagant claims on his behalf. They called him "the everlasting Son of Righteousness," "the fairest of ten thousand," and "the only begotten Son of God," and he failed to remonstrate and to make clear the distinction between himself and the Christ within. His behavior, as distinct from his doctrine, had gone beyond the pale. Later in Bristol, some followers accompanied him as he rode on horseback, strewing garments in the way, and chanting, "Holy, holy, holy, Lord God of Israel." This public adulation Naylor seems to have accepted, if not encouraged. He was promptly imprisoned.

It is true that before the magistrates on the day following he insisted that the title "fairest of ten thousand" was addressed not to himself but to that which the Father had begotten in him. When asked, "Art thou the only Son of God?" he replied: "I am the Son of God, but I have many brethren. . . . Where God is manifest in the flesh, there is the everlasting Son, and I do witness God in the flesh." He did not claim to constitute in his person the second coming of Christ. Rather, he insisted, "The Lord hath made me a sign of His coming, and that honour that belongeth to Christ Jesus in whom I am revealed may be given to Him, as when on earth at Jerusalem, according to the measure." These careful and defensible replies do not suggest madness. We learn from his own testimony that he had been fasting for some fifteen or sixteen days and his judgment may have been impaired by physical exhaustion. His defense was that when he accepted the reverence that can properly be addressed only to the Christ he did so only in the role he was playing on behalf of the Christ and as a sign of the second coming, not in his own right. But later he fully confessed that his behavior had in fact been idolatrous. It was his behavior he repented of, especially in relation to what others said of him. There was little in the way of actual statement which he was obliged to recant.

He submitted with extraordinary courage and stamina to public punishment. He was subjected to floggings of his naked body, the boring through of his tongue with a hot poker, and the branding of his forehead with a "B" (for Blasphemer). On hearing the sentence of physical punishment, he had said calmly: "God has given me a body: God will I hope give me a spirit to endure it. The Lord lay not these things to your charge." He lived up to this aspiration in the event, bearing

himself as nobly under the extremity of physical suffering as any
of the martyrs. Nor has anyone who suffered so severely for
wrongdoing been in the end more free of bitterness. His aberration having been mercifully removed, he could write the immortal lines:

> There is a spirit which I feel that delights to do no evil nor to revenge
> any wrong, but delights to endure all things, in hope to enjoy its own
> in the end. Its hope is to outlive all wrath and contention, and to
> weary out all exaltation and cruelty, or whatever is of a nature
> contrary to itself. It sees to the end of all temptation. As it bears no
> evil in itself, so it conceives none in thoughts to any other. If it be
> betrayed, it bears it, for its ground and spring is in the mercies and
> forgiveness of God. Its crown is weakness, its life is everlasting love
> unfeigned, and takes its kingdom with entreaty and not with conten-
> tion, and keeps it by lowliness of mind. In God also it can rejoice,
> though none else regard it, or can own its life. It's conceived in
> sorrow, and brought forth without any to pit it, nor doth it murmur
> at grief and oppression. It never rejoiceth but through sufferings: for
> with the world's joy it is murdered. I found it alone, being forsaken.
> I have fellowship therein with them who lived in dens and desolate
> places in the earth, who through death obtained this resurrection
> and eternal holy life.[18]

We may identify in James Naylor the besetting temptation
that accompanies a certain type of mystical identification with
the spiritual prototype or archetypal image. We can also see in
him one in whom love and concern and their fruits in tenderness
and humility ultimately prevailed. The sustained moral aberrations that afflicted the Ranters and other historical, mystical
groups follow upon the assumption that under the influence of
or in union with the Spirit one can do no wrong. At the same
time, in Francis of Assisi history has witnessed a form of identification of disciple and master that may even produce the
stigmata without unhinging the mind or corrupting the spirit.

A very basic question is involved. When Paul spoke of the
war within his members in such vivid and convincing terms, "I
do not do the good I want, but the evil I do not want is what
I do," was he speaking of a condition that was permanently
transcended after his conversion or of one that constitutes the

abiding interior plague for all of humanity? Much that George
Fox, and some of the Anabaptists on the Continent, wrote is
open to the interpretation that real conversion was in effect a
permanent entrance into present salvation. Perfection was attainable, not merely a state devoutly to be sought. One must
remember that the state of grace can be maintained only at the
cost of eternal vigilance and sustained obedience. The tempter
is never far to seek and there is no guarantee of immunity.

We have cited the case of James Naylor to illustrate one of
the pitfalls to which the mystical approach to religious experience is prone. Human nature is material for redemption; not in
this life is it ever fully redeemed. Pride goes before a fall. One's
most grievous temptation is always the perversion of one's
greatest talent. There is no greater religious talent than the
mystical faculty; proportionately great is the fall of that person
in whom this talent is subverted by pride, especially the ego
inflation prompted by popular acclaim. Up to a certain point,
Naylor was simply practicing what he preached: the reality of
the indwelling Christ and the power of the life lived in the light
of redemption. To assume that the war within one's members
is over after conversion is fatal. In the twinkling of an eye and
without being aware of what is happening one may be unseated.
Subtle are the temptations to evil which dwell within. And the
condemnation rests upon Naylor not only for having relished
too much the adoration of some of his followers but, perhaps
still more blameworthy, for having unwittingly led them astray.
We are our brothers' keepers whether or not we wish to be,
especially those over whom we exercise influence.

THE DANGERS OF A MYSTICISM OF WITHDRAWAL

Such are some of the dangers of involvement. Another danger to which the psyche of the mystic is prone is noninvolve-
ment. If the mysticism is of the variety that Albert Schweitzer
called life-negating, the temptation may be to opt out of all
responsibility, even avoiding all meaningful relationships. In the
quest for Nirvana in the Eastern religions, the objective was
release not only from desire and attachment but also from the

cycle of transmigration. The aim was escape from "maya," the dance of chance and change, into oblivion, the void, nothingness. By no means is all Eastern mysticism of this life-negating kind. But psychologically it is fair to relate a certain fatalism regarding social and economic conditions to the prevalence of this strain of mystical experience.

In an earlier chapter, I insisted that mysticism may provide the most passionate and sustained motivation for striving toward social change. I was speaking then of the mystical experience of empathic identification with other human beings in their sufferings. But if the aspiration is to step outside the still evolving universe altogether, then the coveted mystical experience constitutes an aberration. It represents withdrawal, renunciation of responsibility, non-being as well as non-becoming. Happily, as we have already related, the greatest of the Eastern mystics, Gautama Buddha, when he might have attained this goal, renounced it in favor of compassionate involvement in teaching others the eightfold way into the holy life.

The West has not been free of the life-negating variety. From the early anchorites, the monastic movements have always harbored some for whom the contemplative life appealed as an escape from the rigors of involvement. The example of Simeon Stylites fortunately strikes the modern mind as not salutary, but pathological. I do not suggest that the mysticism nurtured by the monasteries was predominantly negative. Often the contemplative discipline, cultivated as it was in hours of solitude, was balanced by a salutary communal discipline of ministering to one another according to talent and interest and of venturing forth from the monastery in manifold forms of service. We do, however, meet this vagary of mysticism both within and outside the monastic walls. Wherever and whenever it is observed, the objective seems to be personal salvation, unrelated to the needs of one's brothers. One undertakes the discipline of the contemplative prayer for personal attainment of bliss, not in the spirit in which Jesus practiced obedience: "For their sake I consecrate myself." The admonition of Meister Eckhart is still relevant: if one is wrapped in the ecstasy of contemplation, and his brother has need of his service, he must go at once to that brother's aid, lest he suffer damnation.

The Dangers of Various Types of Hallucination

In our day there are still men and women who are seduced by the false mysticism of withdrawal without intent to return to the responsibilities of common life. Many monasteries languish for promising novices recruited from the world. On the other hand, there is the widespread appeal of the hallucinogenic drugs, especially for the young. It would seem that the same longing for a type of mystical experience is operative here. The common expression for the experience, "going on a trip," is symbolic of an escape into another world while one continues to live in urban America.

Some responsible experimenters like Aldous Huxley have apparently believed that the experience is authentically religious. Huxley seemed to be serious in making the suggestion in his novel *Island* that initiation into a deeper dimension of life might be facilitated by a ceremony for religious humanists in which young men and women could take controlled doses of LSD as a counterpart to the sacrament of confirmation. At the same time, in his own account of his experience under the influence of LSD, he makes an interesting confession. While he was fascinated by the impact made upon him by color represented in a vase of flowers and by nuances of some familiar music to which he had not responded under normal conditions, he was less sensitive to the interior movement of concern for persons—his wife, for example. The same criticism could be leveled at other forms of withdrawal mysticism to which we have already alluded. We need to recognize, however, the striking difference between these aberrations and the classic mysticism of life affirmation whose major product is deeper compassion and more resolute involvement in work for a better life for one's fellows.

This drug-induced experience is analogous to the extent that it temporarily produces perception of interrelatedness and interdependence. But it is also dangerous, since it may produce dissociation or schizophrenia in unstable persons and permanently impair individuation. I have known a number of persons who have claimed to have had religious experiences induced by drugs. I want to be respectful here. It may be that there has been a carry-over into the rest of life in terms of a new sensitivity and perceptiveness. But as far as I can tell, these experiences have not really met the criteria proposed by Rufus Jones: a heightened sense of cohesiveness in the personality and a marked increase in psychic energy thereafter. Nor does passion seem to have been transmuted into compassion, as is characteristic in the alchemy of the authentic experience, unaided by drugs. Joy, if joy has been present, seems confined to the period under the influence of the drug—not to have infused the general quality of life thereafter. The enchantment has not the same staying power, nor is life so permanently informed as a result. Probably this is why so many are irresistibly drawn to experience "one more trip," if they have not fallen into actual addiction.

Some men and women who have been authentic mystics have reported psychic phenomena which in our time would be labeled audio, tactual, or visual hallucination, or a combination of all three. But the wisest of the mystics, even in the Middle Ages, who report experiences of this kind, make it clear that they learned to be wary of them. We should be still more suspicious in our post-Freudian day.

Yet we too dream. We are overtaken by fantasy. We are even encouraged by some modern psychologists to cultivate a process which has been called twilight imaging. What is more, we are urged by hardheaded depth psychologists to be attentive to the images that arise in dreams and fantasy. They may afford what Paul Martin *(Experiment in Depth: A Study of the Work of Jung, Eliot, and Toynbee)* calls "transforming images," from which we can learn a great deal about ourselves and discover directions for current growth. But we are much more aware than were previous generations of the almost infinite possibility of self-deception which confronts anyone who undertakes to fathom his own psyche without the aid of an experienced counselor.

A mystical identification with interior archetypal images like the animus, the anima, and the shadow can be as disastrous as identification with historic messianic figures. It can alter the ego and put one out of touch with reality. The psychic experience of voices and visions may spring from either form of identification. They may convey wise counsel from the unconscious. At the same time, they may never safely be taken at face value or in a literal sense as authentic direct communication from on high. Always the deciphering of a code is involved. The symbolism is invariably complex and one must work at interpretation with the utmost patience and restraint over a long period of time. The objective aid of a trusted analyst or counselor is needed, one who shares the ideals and values while being detached from the particular skein of entanglement. It is indeed, as Paul Martin calls it, an experiment in depth. The depth is such that one may well drown in it without the presence of others who may come to the rescue. On the other hand, the reward of a successful experiment in depth is a return that brings everything together in the thoroughgoing integration that is ultimate integrity.

Using Depth-Psychological Insights to Avoid These Dangers

The mystic way that I am advocating is admittedly full of dangers and pitfalls. When some fish left the sea to venture upon dry land, and reptiles rejected an earthbound existence in a persistent attempt to fly, they were certainly beset by dangers for countless generations. It took time for the new amphibian to develop lungs and for the first birds to sprout wings. We are not only saying that mystical religion of a certain type produces the most deeply satisfying human experience and enables the adept more effectively to serve others. We are conjecturing as well that the cultivation of mystical consciousness is currently the evolving edge for the human species. Despite the vocational hazards it involves, mystical religion is gradually producing, at the patient pace of evolution, I believe, the new man, man's successor, the son of man. The authentic developed mystics who have assayed the steep ascent, while maintaining the precarious balance, are the firstborn among many brethren.

We are better equipped than any previous generation of Christians to join the great explorers in this authentic apostolic succession. We have not only the benefit of the wisdom contained in the Scriptures, charting the course taken by the first mystics in our tradition. We have also the benefit of two thousand years of commentary on those Scriptures, both in written and in experimental form. Mystics in this succession have demonstrated both the aberrations into which one may fall and the consecrated and committed life into which one may be born. Since this mystical way is "the perennial philosophy" and the most universal religious experience, everywhere and always, we now are in a position in this age of communication to study the findings of those in other religious traditions who have undertaken to explore the same hazardous way. Given commitment to a life-affirming form of mysticism, including the prophetic emphasis upon social justice, we have an accumulated treasure of counsel from all the living religions as to what constitutes obedience and disobedience in pursuit of the coveted way. It is a day for "mutual irradiation," as Douglas Steere has described it.

Not only this. As the post-Freudian inheritors of a growing body of depth-psychological insights, we are able more readily to avoid certain forms of self-deception to which the mystical way is susceptible. We are able to distinguish between psychic phenomena and capacity for extrasensory perception, on the one hand, and authentic mystical experience, on the other. We can discern the crucial differences between audio, visual, and tactual hallucination, on the one hand, and a disciplined, objective attention to dreams and the messages that come from the unconscious in the process of twilight imagining, on the other. We know the dangers of overidentification with and possession by the interior animus or anima, the shadow side of our nature, the various archetypal images, as well as of inflation by reason of identification with historic figures upon whom we have unconsciously projected these images. No previous generation has had access to so much knowledge about the complexity of the dangers that await the explorer of the mystical way. Perhaps this is one reason that so many are deterred from embarking upon it.

By the same token, if we are minded and "spirited" to take this inward journey, the very extent of the accumulated knowledge of the complexity and gravity of the dangers may spare us the vagaries and aberrations that have afflicted some mystics in earlier times. Shall we be deterred from an inward journey that promises to lead to a life more abundant by the dangers that beset it? We are more knowledgeable than our forebears of the perils and we have more safeguards against them. I believe that we must sit at the feet of the great mystics, that we may be quickened to follow this narrow way that leads into life.

Part 2

Some Varieties of Christian Mysticism

Chapter V

The Fountainhead: Jesus the Jewish Mystic

In the first four chapters I have presumed to suggest the nature of true religion and to interpret what I believe to be its finest flower in "the mystical way." I have been at pains to recognize the dangers attendant on this way while insisting that we are better prepared than any previous generation to avoid these pitfalls. The central thesis has been that the mystical way, properly understood in evolutionary perspective, represents the way *forward* both for the Christian religion and for the individual in the quest for the life more abundant here and now. Mysticism has been interpreted as the phenomenon of "consciousness-raising" in which we may perceive the thrust of continuing evolution in contemporary man.

JESUS AND THE EVOLVING CHRIST MYTH

It is essential now to point to the source and continuity of the mystical element in the Christian phylum. Mystical experience is vital and compelling only when it is quickened by and understood in the light of an organic community with depth in history. It is my conviction that Christian mysticism which is prepared to allow the Christ myth to continue to evolve, and thereby to assimilate new revelations of truth in contemporary perspectives, has the best chance of inheriting the responsibility of becoming the religion of man in the future.

It is therefore necessary to point out how the characteristics of the mystical way received their charter in the New Testament and have continued to proclaim their authenticity through the apostolic succession of Christian mystics. Christian mysticism begins with Jesus, the Jewish mystic, and is given its earliest forms of expression in Paul and in the author of the Fourth Gospel. In the compass of this small book we cannot hope to follow this apostolic succession through subsequent Christian history. But it will be useful, perhaps, to suggest the variety of Christian mysticism by pointing to three figures—Augustine, Meister Eckhart, and Teilhard de Chardin—as reflecting ancient, medieval, and modern forms of the age-old, universal, and continuing experience.

In my book *Rediscovering the Christ,* I undertook to distinguish between the Jesus of history and the evolving Christ myth, which has always had a life of its own, beginning with its predecessor, the evolving messiah myth in the Old Testament, and extending through successive mutations ever since the apostolic church identified Jesus as the Messiah. I use the word "myth" in the sense defined in the dictionary: "a fabulous narrative founded on some event, especially in the early existence of a people, and embodying their ideas as to their origin, their gods, natural phenomena, etc." It will be necessary here to reflect some of the arguments developed in greater depth in my earlier book in order to suggest that Jesus himself was the first Christian to pursue the mystical way, that in this most important way he was indeed the firstborn among many brethren.

Those persons brought up in the Christian religion who are working their way through to a theology that will keep their world one in this twentieth century will have to face sooner or later the crucial question of how to relate to the Jesus of history and to the Christ myth. Not merely those within the Christian community, but those outside the Christian community, if they are interested at all, will press this question. Moreover, if the evolving Christ myth in the New Testament, in the liturgy and prayer life of the church, has ever been meaningful and made claims upon one's inward capacity for reverence and devotion, there are questions to be asked and answered. One may feel a personal identification with the disciples in that memorable confrontation on the road to Caesarea Philippi when Jesus, having first inquired what others were saying of him, demanded: "But who do you say that I am?" (Mark 8:27).

I have on my desk a small reproduction of one of Rembrandt's portraits of Jesus, the original of which hangs in the Fogg Art Museum at Harvard University. It is one of the few representations of him on canvas that do not disturb me aesthetically. The whole force of expression in the countenance seems to press the urgency of this inquiry. Our initial commitment to a specific meaning for the term "religion" requires of us a binding together in a new bundle of the pieces of experience and reflection that we have. For those of us who still relate to the Christian church, a plausible place must be found for the Jesus of history and the Christ myth.

THE CENTRAL SPECIFICATION FOR A MODERN CHRISTOLOGY

Over the last thirty years I have had to bind into my own sheaf of accumulating experiences and reflections the fact of evolution. This involved the necessity of assimilating into any viable theology this all-encompassing new perspective on human existence. You will recall Teilhard's proclamation: "Evolution is a general condition to which all theories, all hypotheses, all systems must bow and which they must satisfy henceforward if they are to be thinkable and true. Evolution is a light illuminating all facts, a curve that all lines must follow." When this premise is taken seriously, one perceives that this is in truth a new light illuminating all facts. It is not so much a case of assimilating this fact into one's theology as one's theology being transformed by the perception of its implications.

The church's ancient myth of creation had to be radically reshaped in this new light. This in large measure has been done. But Christianity's most distinctive myth, that of the incarnation, the fountainhead, in a sense, from which all other Christian doctrines flow, has not yet been brought fully into focus under this more than ultraviolet ray. To relate the need to Teilhard's other image, we must confess, I believe, that the lines of our

Christology (our response to Jesus' question) have not yet begun to follow that curve.

We are afforded at another point in Teilhard's *The Phenomenon of Man* what we might take as the central specification for building a new concept:

> What makes and classifies a "modern man" (and a whole host of our contemporaries is not yet "modern" in this sense) is having become capable of seeing in terms not of space and time alone, but also of duration, or—and it comes to the same thing—of biological space-time; and above all having become incapable of seeing anything otherwise—anything—*not even himself.*[19]

I do not pretend to understand the implications this statement must hold for a physicist, a biologist, or a philosopher. But I do feel an overriding need to become a modern man, with any and all risks this might involve, and to be able to communicate to other modern men and women what I still believe in a new sense to be glorious good news. What this specification says to me is that I must understand Jesus of Nazareth in the light of the process of evolution. The moral and intellectual imperative I draw from this statement is that we must become capable of seeing "in terms . . . of biological space-time" and of becoming "incapable of seeing anything otherwise"—and here I add, not even the Jesus of history.

THE QUEST OF THE HISTORICAL JESUS

In the latter part of the last century, contemporaneously with the new evolutionary insight, there arose a succession of scholars in Germany who undertook a critical analysis of the Bible. This involved critical study of the life of Jesus. In 1906, Albert Schweitzer reviewed the work that had been done and offered his own original findings. His book (English translation entitled *The Quest of the Historical Jesus,* 1910) made a tremendous impact upon theological thought. It was a monumental achievement and marked perhaps the first great step in the direction of seeing Jesus in terms of biological space-time. It distinguished the various currents of thought that played upon Jesus inwardly and determined the main lines of his own self-identification. It stressed the importance of Jesus' time-bound misconception of a swiftly approaching apocalyptic end of the times. It drew attention to subsequent confluence of Greek ideas through Paul and John, and the transformation by the church of the Jesus of history into the Christ of faith. Yet at the close of that book it is to the Christ of faith rather than the Jesus of history that Schweitzer pointed.

> He comes to us as One unknown, without a name, as of old, by the lake-side, He came to those men who knew Him not. He speaks to us the same word: "Follow thou me!" and sets us to the tasks which He has to fulfil for our time. He commands. And to those who obey Him, whether they be wise or simple, He will reveal Himself in the toils, the conflicts, the sufferings which they shall pass through in His fellowship, and as an ineffable mystery, they shall learn in their own experience Who He is.[20]

At the beginning of his book, Schweitzer made a humble confession and a prophetic prediction:

> We have not yet arrived at any reconciliation between history and modern thought—only between half-way history and half-way thought. What the ultimate goal towards which we are moving will be, what this something is which shall bring new life and new regulative principles to coming centuries, we do not know. We can only dimly divine that it will be the mighty deed of some mighty original genius, whose truth and rightness will be proved by the fact that we, working at our poor half thing, will oppose him might and main—we who imagine we long for nothing more eagerly than a genius powerful enough to open up with authority a new path for the world, seeing that we cannot succeed in moving it forward along the track which we have so laboriously prepared.[21]

We are presuming now to suggest that Teilhard may be one in a succession of such geniuses. The new path that is being opened up with authority is the very biological space-time perspective to which we have referred as the major specification. C. G. Jung may well be another in the succession. Perhaps the recognition by Schweitzer that no one had as yet succeeded in making an adequate reconciliation between history and modern thought, but only between "half-way history and half-way thought," was also an accurate judgment upon his own work. His tribute to German scholarship is still moving: "in the study of the life of Jesus it was working for the future—in pure faith in the truth, not seeing whereunto it wrought."[22] We see evidence, however, of his own "half-way history" and "half-way thought" when he wrote:

> It is only at first sight that the absolute indifference of early Christianity towards the life of the historical Jesus is disconcerting. When Paul, representing those who recognise the signs of the times, did not desire to know Christ after the flesh, that was the first expression of the impulse of self-preservation by which Christianity continued to be guided for centuries. It felt that with the introduction of the historic Jesus into its faith, there would arise something new, something which had not been foreseen in the thoughts of the Master Himself, and that thereby a contradiction would be brought to light, the solution of which would constitute one of the great problems of the world.[23]

Schweitzer felt that primitive Christianity was therefore right to focus attention on the future, on the second coming of the Christ, and to play down the historical Jesus. By bequeathing Gospels instead of biographies, the early Christians gave us the Idea, the Word, the Christ myth, and diverted us from legitimate historical questions. This development may have been necessary to establish and preserve the church. But it succeeded in dropping a curtain upon the Jesus of history which the modern mind has its own peculiar compulsion to lift. Schweitzer traces for us the whole subsequent development until the late nineteenth century with a single stroke of his pen:

> The supra-mundane Christ and the historical Jesus of Nazareth had to be brought together into a single personality at once historical and raised above time. That was accomplished by Gnosticism and the Logos Christology. Both, from opposite standpoints, because they were seeking the same goal, agreed in sublimating the historical Jesus into the supra-mundane Idea.[24]

In this way, after the eschatological promise had to be progressively abandoned, all interest in investigating the life of the historical personality was also laid down.

And so it remained, until the new need to trace critically the development itself arose by the prompting of the post-Darwinian era—the end of which is not yet. Following the work of Schweitzer there began in Germany, during the First World War, another development, the so-called *Formgeschichte,* or Form Criticism, school. This was an attempt to reach behind the various written sources in the New Testament to the oral tradition before the Gospels as reflected in certain literary forms to be found in them. It was hoped through these to come closer to the acts and sayings of Jesus. Though intended to serve as a tool of historical research, this emphasis resulted in fact in a transfer of interest from the Jesus of history to the Jesus in early Christian thought. The chief contribution of this school was the delineation of the main lines of the kerygma, the primitive message about Jesus the Christ that was preached in the earliest church, before the New Testament came to be written. This helped to reconstruct the history of theology about Jesus the Christ in the earliest period, but it was disappointing as far as helping us to recover the historical Jesus.

This movement was followed by a new emphasis on what came to be called Biblical Theology. It presupposes that there is only one basic Biblical theology, though there were of course many authors writing over a span of a thousand years. It argued that there is continuity and consistency in what has been called a salvation view of history as a succession of the mighty acts of God, culminating in the advent of Jesus, his death, and the experiences of the resurrection. "God spoke of old to our fathers by the prophets; but in these last days he has spoken to us by a Son" (Heb. 1:1). We may be helped by the study of Biblical theology to understand elements of thought which Jesus inherited and was influenced by. But, as Henry Cadbury points out in his *The Eclipse of the Historical Jesus,* "the Jesus of theology begins at the point in time where the Jesus of history leaves off."[25] These very statements about the acts of God in Christ before the New Testament canon closed put the historical figure in some sense beyond our reach.

Dr. Cadbury wrote further:

> Modern biblical theology shows a continuation of the same desire to enjoy the assets of historical anchorage without too much concern for the difficult and partly hopeless task of recovering the actual portrait of Jesus. . . . The Christological discussions of subsequent centuries were not based on historical evidence but on philosophical deductions from the mere premise of the incarnation.[26]

There is this unending and inevitable conflict between the theologian and the historian. Committed as he is to the vocation of historian, Dr. Cadbury saw the tension in these terms:

> The influence of theology on the quest of the historical Jesus is that today as always theology tends to deflect attention from the subject. It is aware that it is doing so. But it does not care. . . .
>
> The historians and the theologians have a different sense of values. The latter think their sphere, the dramatic portrayal of human experience, is more relevant. They regard history as useless. They quite correctly gauge the difficulty of recovering Jesus. . . . They can claim that the Jesus of history has never been central in Christianity.[27]

Hence, one of the most important of these Biblical theologians, Rudolf Bultmann, insists on demythologizing the cosmology of the New Testament. At the same time he is content to accept the Christ myth in terms of a response in faith to the kerygma. He insists that one not only cannot but must not go behind the Christ here portrayed to the Jesus of history. He puts it this way:

> Jesus Christ confronts men nowhere other than in the *kerygma*, as he had so confronted Paul and brought him to decision. The *kerygma* does not mediate historical knowledge [of Jesus] and one may not seek to get beyond the *kerygma* and use it to reconstruct the historical Jesus. That would be the Christ according to the flesh of the past. Not the historical Jesus, but Jesus Christ, the preached Christ, is the Lord.[28]

So Bultmann ends up virtually where Schweitzer did. Post-Bultmannians, notably Günther Bornkamm and James M. Robinson, have renewed the quest of the historical Jesus. But none has yet fully come free of his own theological precommitments.

THE JESUS OF HISTORY
FROM THE PERSPECTIVE OF BIOLOGICAL SPACE-TIME

The crucial fact of our time for me is that our post-Darwinian perspective, our modern distinctive way of seeing everything in terms of biological space-time, has simply ruled out the whole commitment to so-called Biblical theology of salvation history through the mighty acts of God as the only source of revelation. I must try to indicate carefully what I mean. "Salvation history" predicates that after the creation in which God saw everything he had made and beheld that it was "very good," there ensued a "fall of man" which must have made man's place in it seem suddenly "very bad." It became necessary for this same transcendent, "above and beyond history," God to initiate certain mighty acts whose purpose was the re-creation, or remaking, of man. At length, following a number of mighty acts recorded in the Old Testament, he entered the plane of history in person in Jesus Christ.

This view of history, I believe, is no longer tenable in its own terms in the light of our knowledge of the fact of evolution. When one feels constrained to see everything from an evolutionary rather than merely a historical perspective, one cannot accept the myth of the fall as it has come to us. As a metaphor of an ever repeated existential failure to realize our best aspirations and hopes, a "fall" from what we believe we have it in us to become, yes! But not a fall from anything we ever were! There may have been a "moment" of innocence, when, emerging from a lower form of life, we did not yet realize the gift of moral choice that developing reflection and conscience had bestowed upon us. But no one can honestly look upon that state as a higher one than the potential nobility of choosing the right when wrong beguiles so irresistibly.

The first axiom then is this: Evolution attests that up to now,

as far as the line of descent of man is concerned, all the way back
to the molecular combination that produced cellular substance,
it has indeed been a case of onward and upward through ever
more wonderful unity in ever greater complexity. When one's
scale of observation is evolution, one perceives there has been
in man's descent (or, more properly, ascent) unbroken progress.
The creation is unfinished. In Michelangelo's great visual image,
the finger of the creator God has not yet finally been withdrawn
from the unfinished man. The transposition we must make in
our thought, however, is not to think of that finger as touching
man from outside, but as reaching up through the evolutionary
process and still shaping from within the mind and conscience
of man.

The second axiom drawn from this perspective is that forward movement has always come first through the individual.
A new species emerges gradually through a succession of
"sports" or mutations incarnate in individuals until a new strain
is produced. The modern man as defined by Teilhard looks
therefore for salvation not in terms of intervention in history by
a God who is external to it, but by the evolutionary emergence
of the new man whose very being carries the Word to other men.
History is a miniature segment of evolution, the last few seconds
of its time span. Evolution *is* history, writ large. He can look
with equanimity on history because he believes it is borne by a
process in which he has come to have confidence and which he
believes is gradually projecting upon the field of history the
character of the new man. This enthusiasm for man, and this
is a form of humanism, is tamed by the metaphor, also drawn
from evolution, of the possibility of extinction, in this case, for
the first time, self-willed extinction. But he finds it hard to
believe that something so beautiful as the human personality at
its best, from which we draw our ultimate values, whose antece-
dents have so precariously preserved the unemptied chalice of
potential for so long, should finally disappear from the face of
the earth, even from the countenance of the universe.

This second axiom points to the fact that man's continuing
evolution is taking place now before our very eyes. The movement is so slow in relation to the span of our lives that we are

not aware of it. Nevertheless by projection forward of the process we can read in the records of evolution in the past, we can
see that individuals will arise who contain within their persons
the secret of the next advance in man's evolution. Now it is a
presumption, which many will consider unjustified, to suggest
that this growing edge of the new man is precisely his mystical
or contemplative capacity as we have defined it, and that the
great mystics are the sports, the forerunners not only of the new
man but of the new age. In them, conscience has caught up with
intelligence by virtue of the mystical capacity of identification
and the sustained practice of loving that of God in others as they
love that of God in themselves. Of course this is conjecture,
definitely not scientifically demonstrable! But it is a hypothesis
I believe to be tenable. And for me it has meant a new orientation that has made all the difference.

It is precisely from this set of presuppositions that I am
suggesting we take a new look at the historical Jesus. I know full
well the dangers involved in the possible projection of unconscious subjective elements. Bruce Barton saw Jesus as a super-
salesman, and Ernest Renan saw him as a romantic. Others have
seen him as a lawgiver and judge. Everyone's answer to the
persistent question, "But who do you say that I am?" is likely
to be given in terms of one's own preoccupation or unrecognized
need. I know, too, that there is a real sense in which the Jesus
of history is quite beyond our recovery, and we are likely therefore to force the facts to fit our preconceptions and precommitments. Undoubtedly, this reconstruction will be in some degree
guilty of both. Yet the presumption, it seems to me, is justified
as an honest attempt "to reconcile history and modern
thought," to use the terms of Albert Schweitzer—or to look at
the Jesus of history and the Christ of theology from the perspective of the modern mind Teilhard identifies for us.

From our appraisal of the nature of religion and of the significance of mystical religion expressed in the earlier chapters, you
will see at once why, from the perspective of biological space-
time, Jesus emerges for me as primarily a Jewish mystic. I
believe that he was the greatest mystic the world has yet known
in the sense of the sustained practice of perceiving the presence

of God in himself, in nature, and in others, and in the practice of obedience to what he understood to be the will of that God. That he was the greatest of the prophets follows almost as a corollary, a prophet of the Kingdom of God on earth.

Such a view, I believe, meets the central specification of a viable Christology for modern man. It begins by insisting upon the full humanity of Jesus and limits any view as to his divinity to a difference of degree, rather than of kind, from other men. All are made in the image of God. There is that of God in every person. In Jesus of Nazareth more of God shone through and was realized than in any other. This approach preserves the concept of an unbroken evolutionary continuity which, it seems to me, is the first requirement of a modern view of Jesus. At the same time, if the claim that he is the greatest of the mystics can be plausibly supported, and if it be further accepted that the mystical capacity is the growing edge of continuing evolution in man, then it would appear that he is indeed the "Son of Man" in the sense of the new man, man's successor, the firstborn among many brethren. Moreover, from this perspective, his incalculable influence upon the rest of mankind can be accounted for on other grounds than the church's historic doctrine of divinity.

When an animal is evolving toward some new capacity—let us say a reptile is straining toward flight—the new species is produced by a succession of heroic individual efforts over many millennia. Constant trial and failure, and renewed effort, persists until a breakthrough comes. Must it not be the same with man? With animals the movement forward is unconscious, below the level of sentience. But with man there can be awareness of what is going on in the context of biological space-time. We should look for the evolving faculty in the area of some new form of consciousness, because we know that man's ascent has been marked thus far by new forms of consciousness. The mystical is just emerging, it would appear, when the scale of observation is evolution. Moreover, its vivid presence in any individual would inevitably evoke a response in others in whom the latent capacity was only partially awakened. When Jesus is reported to have said, "You will not know who I am except the Father reveal it to you," we might interpret this word from our perspective as saying in effect: "Only a corresponding faculty in you can confirm the divinity of the way of life I represent to you." The birth of the Christ life in Jesus of Nazareth can, as the mystic Meister Eckhart insisted, quicken the noble birth of the life of the soul within others, that is, the seed of the Christ life in them.

I am suggesting that the inwardness of Jesus' experience was precisely the mystical, existential sense of unity with God, the Absolute, the Ultimate, the One. For the Nazarene this would inevitably be understood as unity with the God of Judaism whom he had described as a loving Father. This is the basic mystical experience that lies behind his understanding of his own vocation, whether or not he believed himself to be the Messiah in any sense. Of the many varying and even conflicting images of the Messiah, he inclined toward the suffering servant image in the fifty-third chapter of Isaiah. He understood from this prophetic utterance and his mystical experience on the Mount that obedience would lead to the cross, and he was at pains to prepare his disciples for that eventual outcome. Albert Schweitzer's argument that he felt he would also return to inaugurate the Kingdom is, I think, incontrovertible, whether or not he identified himself as the traditional Messiah. We cannot know to what extent an acceptance of the messianic role was part of his inner self-identification and to what extent it was foisted upon him by the disciples after his death and the experiences of resurrection appearances. But the mystical consciousness of interior identification with God and with his fellows through obedience to the will of God—this stands and retains abiding significance for all men. This will be further interpreted in the chapter on the God-mysticism of the Fourth Gospel (the supreme portrait of Jesus the Jewish mystic by another Jewish mystic).

Finally, it remains to be pointed out that the concepts of divinity, imposed on the historical Jesus by the pious imagination of the church, have actually kept us from seeing him primarily as the Jewish mystic he was, and from fully appreciating his abiding significance in evolutionary perspective. Quite apart from the historical Jesus, all men have, in Jungian terms, an archetypal image of perfect humanity, an animus figure, projected, if you will, from the unconscious. How much of this idealized dream of the perfect man, of what it would be like to be one who had fully realized the human potential, has been projected upon the historical Jesus, through the evolving doctrine of his divinity, we shall never know. But it is time that we abandon what may well be the most persistent idolatry for Christians, one that Jesus himself counseled against, namely, that which would make Jesus into God.

We must also distinguish between the historical figure and the archetypal image of the Godlike man, between Jesus and the Christ myth which has continued to haunt the fantasy, the dreams, and the aspirations of Christians. We can speak of the Christ if we choose, the archetypal image of the perfect man, that which shone through the historical Jesus, and can be born and nourished in us, in some measure at least. It is this for which we must look in ourselves and in others. As Christians we find in the historical figure of Jesus in the Gospels—especially, I think, in John—all the authentic marks that will enable us to recognize the divine image. In this sense we may continue to participate in the Christian myth. But I believe the time has come, in order to enter into genuine dialogue with our Jewish brethren and those of other living religions as well as to come to a better understanding of our own, when we must forgo limiting identification of the archetypal Christ image to Jesus. We must begin to think of the indwelling Christ or God-man in all men, pointing the way to a new humanity and to the ideal community, the Kingdom of God on earth.

If neither Teilhard de Chardin nor C. G. Jung is precisely the "mighty original genius" predicted by Albert Schweitzer who will "reconcile for us history and modern thought," they may well be among a succession of such geniuses. Teilhard saw the evolutionary significance of that divine image as it was reflected in the historical Jesus. But in his working out of the metaphor of the point omega as the ultimate "Christification" of the universe, he unfortunately used a term whose connotations are too much bound to one great historical religious tradition. Nevertheless, through the scope of the evolutionary process which he

envisaged on a cosmic scale, we have been able to see the significance of the image of God in man as we have never seen it
before. For him this image was and remained Jesus the Christ.
For the Christian the image will always relate to the historical
figure of Jesus and be judged by his life. But it must be released
from further fixation of this kind if we are now to move forward
in dialogue with the other great living religions, and more effectively bind into one bundle the experience and knowledge of a
modern man.

At the close of the last of his books to be translated, Teilhard
has prophetic counsel: "The Age of Nations is past. The task
before us now, if we would not perish, is to build the earth." Is
it not also true that the age of competing faiths is past? The task
before us, if we would not perish spiritually, is to build religion
by furthering the mystical approach to religious experience.
This does not mean to create a new eclectic religion, nor abandon the organic historic continuum of his own religion. It does
mean a new capacity to see analogies, to universalize by seeing
all dogmas and doctrines as metaphors that point to realities
others may see in other terms. Above all, for the Christian, it
means seeing both the historical Jesus and the Christ myth in
terms of biological space-time and depth psychology.

When one does this, the Jesus of history emerges primarily
as a Jewish mystic. What would appear either arrogance and
inflation or paranoia in the discourses attributed to Jesus in the
Fourth Gospel becomes the acceptable reflection of the mystic's
inward experience in depth-psychological terms. The Jesus of
history shines through, plausibly, as a man. He speaks, "in
kind," as all mystics in all ages have spoken, but "in degree" of
intensity and sustained, existential living in the Kingdom, as no
one, not even the mystics, has ever spoken.

Chapter VI

The Christ-Mysticism of Paul the Apostle

In his book *The Mysticism of Paul the Apostle,* Albert Schweitzer gives us the most penetrating analysis we possess of the mysticism of Paul. This mysticism, apart from that of Jesus himself, is the earliest in the apostolic succession of Christian mystics. One recognizes that Schweitzer's own Christ-mysticism derives its chief inspiration from this source.

In the closing chapter, Schweitzer pays lyric tribute to the apostle's achievement as a thinker and as a mystic. The author's unconscious identification with Paul, at least in aspiration, is unmistakable:

Paul vindicated for all time the rights of thought in Christianity. Above belief which drew its authority from tradition, he set the knowledge which came from the Spirit of Christ. There lives in him an unbounded and undeviating reverence for truth. He will consent only to a limitation of liberty laid on him by the law of love, not to one imposed by doctrinal authority. . . . The result of this first appearance of thought in Christianity is calculated to justify, for all periods, the confidence that faith has nothing to fear from thinking, even when the latter disturbs its peace and raises a debate which appears to promise no good results for the religious life. . . . It is the thoughts of the Apostle of the Gentiles, who was opposed by the faith of his own time, which have again and again acted as a power of renewal in the faith of subsequent periods. . . . Christianity can only become the living truth for successive generations if thinkers constantly arise within it who, in the spirit of Jesus, make belief in Him capable of intellectual apprehension in the thought-forms of the world-view proper to their time. . . . Paul is the patron-saint of thought in Christianity.[29]

DISTINCTION BETWEEN PRIMITIVE AND DEVELOPED MYSTICISM

At the outset in this study, performed at the peak of his varied talents, Schweitzer draws a distinction between primitive and developed mysticism. As a general characteristic of all mystics he identifies the peculiar capacity of "looking upon the division between earthly and super-earthly, temporal and eternal, as transcended, and feeling [oneself], while still externally earthly and temporal, to belong to the super-earthly and eternal."[30] In primitive mysticism the experience of the super-earthly and eternal takes place by means of a "mystery," a magical act through which identification with a divine being is realized. This is true not only in quite primitive religions but also in the Greek mystery religions. Only when the conception of the universal is reached and the objective is not union with a particular divine being but with Being itself can a specific mysticism be considered developed. In this case the identification with the super-earthly and eternal is realized, not by some magical act of ceremony, but through an act of thinking. This "intellectual mysticism" is to be found in individual mystics in all the great living religions, in Platonism and Stoicism, and in certain philosophers like Spinoza, Schopenhauer, and Hegel who belong to no particular school.

The mysticism of Paul, according to Schweitzer, lies somewhere between primitive and intellectual mysticism. "In Paul there is no God-mysticism; only a Christ-mysticism by means of which man comes into relation to God."[31] He speaks of sonship to God, but not of union with God. Of course for Paul, Jesus and the Christ were inseparably one. So also for Schweitzer. Therefore in this chapter I shall refer to Jesus and the Christ indiscriminately, asking the reader to bear in mind the distinction I insist on making for myself.

Paul's distinctive phrase for describing the essence of the

mystical experience is "being-in-Christ." This is brought about
by a process of having died and risen again with him, through
which the participant has been released from bondage to sin and
the law and set free to possess the Spirit of Christ that assures
resurrection. Among the texts that bear testimony to the experience, here are a few of the most vivid:

> For I through the law died to the law, that I might live to God. I
> have been crucified with Christ; it is no longer I who live, but Christ
> who lives in me. (Gal. 2:19–20)

> Therefore, if any one is in Christ, he is a new creation; the old has
> passed away, behold, the new has come. (II Cor. 5:17)

> The death he died he died to sin, once for all, but the life he lives
> he lives to God. So you also must consider yourselves dead to sin
> and alive to God in Christ Jesus. (Rom. 6:10–11)

Thus, in Paul, the sonship to God, to which Jesus pointed
his disciples, occurs through being-in-Christ. Schweitzer suggests that Paul is the only Christian thinker in whom Christ-
mysticism is not accompanied by God-mysticism. This, I think,
is an exaggeration. But it is true that Paul remained firmly
rooted in Judaism, for which God-mysticism had always been
suspect as blasphemy. Though Paul has sometimes been represented as a "Hellenist," Schweitzer is at great pains to document
his claim that the theology of Paul was thoroughly Hebraic.
Striking to the marrow of reality in the time-bound limitations
of his Jewish eschatological perspective, he was able to penetrate
the essence of the mystical experience in such a way as to
stimulate others to reinterpret it in the language of another
world view. The greatness of his thought was the inherent universal dimension which enabled it to constitute a bridge to the
Hellenistic conceptions enshrined in the Fourth Gospel in
which a being-in-Christ becomes the means of being-in-God.
But for Paul, while possession of the spirit of Christ is synony-
mous with the Spirit of God, the being-in-Christ never becomes
a being-in-God. The author of the book of Acts, it is true,
represents Paul as saying to the Athenians of God, "In him we
live and move and have our being." But this has the ring of an

attributed Stoic mysticism; in his own writing there is no hint of this direct "God-mysticism."

THE ESCHATOLOGICAL ELEMENT

Paul's own world view is limited by the late Jewish eschatology, that is, ideas concerning the end of the age. He can go this far: "For from him and through him and to him are all things" (Rom. 11:36). But he does not go beyond this, as would Stoic mysticism, and say: "All things are in God." There is in the Stoic strain a static quality compared with the dynamic mysticism of Paul. God-mysticism will be a future reality in the Kingdom; Christ-mysticism, the dying and rising again in Christ, is that which both brings the Kingdom and serves as the guarantor of admission. This dying and rising, moreover, is not merely metaphorical, but is a simple reality experienced in actual fact. Hence Paul nowhere uses the metaphor of "rebirth." Moreover, the dying and rising is not accomplished by the will of the individual, but is predestined for the elect. For these chosen from baptism onward, the dying and rising is an ever renewed experience. Here we see that Paul's is also a sacramental mysticism. The dying and rising, initiated by baptism, makes possible the fellowship with the Christ which is effected through the sacrament of the Lord's Supper. This sacramental life is bound up for Paul with the expectation of the end of the world. It is this characteristic, more than any other, which makes the mysticism of Paul absolutely unique because in it are bound together the nonmystical Jewish eschatology and Christ-mysticism.

Behind all conceptualized mysticism, there is the initial experience. For Paul this took place on the road to Damascus. As with all mystical experience, there is the complex antecedent interior drama of conflict of which the mystical experience is the resolution. Driven by compulsion to be a Pharisee of the Pharisees, more obedient to the letter of the law than any other Jew, Paul yet knew that there was that within his members which was at war with this passionately willed obedience. Moreover, this higher law of love, superseding the old law, strangely drew him. He longed for release from the law which so tormented him and, in the depths of his being, wistfully reflected upon the meaning of the new law. The more he doubted the efficacy of this fierce discipline, the more intense became the self-punishment and the Puritan readiness to stand in judgment upon and to persecute those who put the temptation in the way.

The final unbearable confrontation was reached when, compulsively, he was driven to aid and abet the stoning of Stephen. The sight of that man, who in his dying agony could look with love upon his persecutors and say, "Lord, do not hold this sin against them," was the depth charge that did its quiet work in the soul of Paul. The explosion, the conversion, took place on the Damascus road. It was Jesus the Christ in Stephen whom Paul had been persecuting. Now and henceforth the healing would come by the willed presence of the living Christ within his own being. The expression that his Christ-mysticism found in words thereafter was but the "radiation," as Schweitzer describes it, of "the energy which was henceforth concentrated in his soul" as a result of this experience.

This new experience had to be placed within the context of Paul's world view. The dominant strain in this world view was the Jewish eschatology which was singularly unmystical. The full power of Paul's intellectual capacity was needed to work this miracle of synthesis. The fulfillment of the Jewish eschatological dream had been first identified in his mind with the immediate return of Jesus, the judgment, and the messianic glory these would usher in. Over and over again the Lord's song was sung in the foreign land:

> To wait for his Son from heaven, whom he raised from the dead, Jesus . . . delivers us from the wrath to come. (I Thess. 1:10)

> So that he may establish your hearts unblamable in holiness before our God and Father, at the coming of our Lord Jesus with all his saints. (I Thess. 3:13)

> Who gave himself for our sins to deliver us from the present evil age. (Gal. 1:4)

When Jesus returns, the elect who have "fallen asleep" in him, and those who are still alive, will be transformed into a mode of being appropriate to the Kingdom. At this time even nature will pass through a transformation from a mortal to an immortal state. Meantime, even in this interim period, the law, which had been given by the angels, is invalidated, because of the death of Jesus through which the angels have lost their former power. The law had held that whosoever "hangeth on a tree" is accursed, but Jesus was not accursed, therefore the law is no longer valid. It is precisely on the cross that the law, for Paul, has been annulled. But this means that in some sense the Kingdom has already begun, since, beginning with Christ's death, the law is no longer in effect. It is the projection of the mystical element into the purely eschatological context in Paul that enables redemption to be a present reality for the believer, rather than merely a future one.

The dying and rising process is required for entrance into the Kingdom by eschatological standards. But through mystical identification with Jesus' own death and resurrection, the elect need not pass through a literal counterpart. On Jesus' return they will take up residence immediately in the Kingdom, because, indeed, in the mystical union they have already entered it. Between the resurrection of Jesus and his coming again the transient world and the eternal world are intermingled for the believer. The process set in motion in Paul's own mystical experience on the road to Damascus found reconciliation with his inherited Jewish eschatology in this fashion.

THE CHRIST-MYSTICISM INHERENT IN JESUS' TEACHING

After all, could Jesus not claim that his preaching encouraged a Christ-mysticism? Not only did Jesus proclaim a coming Kingdom; he insisted that the fellowship experienced between his disciples and himself was a foretaste of that to be enjoyed in the Kingdom with the Son of Man. To be sure, there is an element of mystery in this inasmuch as the disciples do not know that Jesus himself is the one who will return as the Son of Man. Nevertheless, the only thing that is essential is that they understand that fellowship with him now will bring about fellowship with the Son of Man in the Kingdom. Moreover, suffering with him now brings, as reward, glory with the Son of Man in the messianic age to come.

> Blessed are you when men revile you and persecute you and utter all kinds of evil against you falsely on my account. Rejoice and be glad, for your reward is great in heaven. (Matt. 5:11–12)

> For whoever would save his life will lose it, and whoever loses his life for my sake will save it. (Matt. 16:25)

The mysticism of Jesus extends still further into the dimension of mystery. The proper understanding of the feeding of the five thousand by the lake may well be as a sacramental meal, not to satisfy hunger, which would make it a physical miracle, but as a table fellowship like that to be enjoyed with the Son of Man in the future. Moreover, this demand of fellowship with him is fulfilled when anyone receives a child in his name, when he feeds the hungry, gives drink to the thirsty, entertains the stranger, clothes the naked, visits the sick and those in prison. Ethical action of itself establishes mystical fellowship, even when the individual is unaware of it. In a sense deeper than blood relationship, those are his mother and his brethren who do the will of God. Men and women are thus encouraged to practice a form of Christ-mysticism before they understand that he who was with them was the Messiah and was to be the Son of Man. Some scholars have thought that Jesus deliberately tried in advocating baptism by spirit as well as water to bring the disciples to the kind of mystical experience that had visited him at baptism.

THE UNION: A PRESENT REALITY

With Jesus' death, a changed situation prevailed. The Christ-mysticism of Paul the apostle has necessarily to be interpreted in terms both more specific and more complex. Others were urging confession of belief in the messiahship of Jesus, looking toward the future realization of unity with him in an age to come. The distinctive emphasis of Paul was to assert the experienced reality of this unity *now*, in this period between the resurrection and the return, as the only badge of assurance of its future reality. It is open to believers *now* to enter into the resurrection mode of existence, before the general resurrection of the dead who "sleep in him." They are able to appropriate the death and resurrection of Jesus in such a way as to undergo *now* their own appointed death and resurrection, while they yet live. When Jesus returns, they will receive at his hands the resurrection state without any interim state, because they are in fact already there. The eschatology of Jesus and the eschatology of Paul are basically one; there are only such minor changes as are necessitated by the post-resurrection and pre-messianic period in which Paul is living. And he could claim that his Christ-mysticism is, in reality, only a recasting of that which Jesus had already conceived and encouraged in relation to his followers.

That Paul's mysticism is a combination of the primitive and the developed forms is seen in the fact that it is through the sacrament of Baptism that faith in the Christ becomes a being-in-Christ. This being-in-Christ is admission into the mystical body of Christ, the community of God. Such men have ceased to be "in the flesh" or "to walk in the flesh," since the flesh has been crucified with Jesus.

> And those who belong to Christ Jesus have crucified the flesh with its passions and desires. (Gal. 5:24)

Their bodies may grow older and be less resilient; but the life of the spirit becomes more intensely alive.

> So we do not lose heart. Though our outer nature is wasting away, our inner nature is being renewed every day. (II Cor. 4:16–17)

This membership in the mystical body of Christ transforms the believer in thought and action. This Christ-mysticism is not an escape from the world but is a means of living in it while one keeps oneself unspotted from it. For Paul, this union with Christ is not so metaphysical as it is physical; his favorite metaphor for it is the bodily union between man and wife. Indeed, an unbelieving husband or wife is sanctified by the belief of the mate.

If any brother has a wife who is an unbeliever, and she consents to live with him, he should not divorce her. If any woman has a husband who is an unbeliever, and he consents to live with her, she should not divorce him. For the unbelieving husband is consecrated through his wife, and the unbelieving wife is consecrated through her husband. Otherwise, your children would be unclean, but as it is they are holy. (I Cor. 7:12–14)

On the other hand, intercourse with a prostitute severs the participant from the community.

Do you not know that he who joins himself to a prostitute becomes one body with her? (I Cor. 6:16)

The characteristically physical, bodily nature of this mystical union as conceived by Paul is further illustrated by the fact that participation in the heathen sacrificial feasts produces a union with demons that is antithetical to union with Christ and nullifies membership in the body of Christ.

I do not want you to be partners with demons. You cannot drink the cup of the Lord and the cup of demons. You cannot partake of the table of the Lord and the table of demons. (I Cor. 10:20–21)

Now, a question arises. When one has sinned after baptism, how does one recover union with the mystical body of Christ? The answer is that atonement, at-one-ment, is secured by suffering with Christ. Paul thought of himself as foremost in his capacity for this kind of suffering:

I will all the more gladly boast of my weaknesses, that the power of Christ may rest upon me. For the sake of Christ, then, I am content with weaknesses, insults, hardships, persecutions, and calamities; for when I am weak, then I am strong. (II Cor. 12:9–20)

For Paul, the place that keeping the law had for Judaism is taken by faith in the redemptive power of the death of Jesus Christ.

There is therefore now no condemnation for those who are in Christ Jesus. For the law of the Spirit of life in Christ Jesus has set me free from the law of sin and death. (Rom. 8:1–2)

In an effort to make this equation clear to the believer, he interprets faith as a form of "doing" which exactly corresponds with the old obedience to the law. He is even at pains to compose a new phrase to make this clear, "obedience to the faith," that the "law of faith" may be juxtaposed to the "law of works." He refers to Jesus the Christ:

> Through whom we have received grace and apostleship to bring about the obedience of faith for the sake of his name among all the nations. (Rom. 1:5)

OBEDIENCE TO FAITH INSTEAD OF LAW

Paul had to fight for this conception of obedience to faith instead of the law against Judaizers who could quote Scripture galore on the other side. Happily he could bring two passages to bear in his favor:

> And he believed the LORD; and he reckoned it to him as righteousness. (Gen. 15:6)

> The righteous shall live by his faith. (Hab. 2:4)

With a high-handedness not altogether uncharacteristic, Paul is quite prepared to bestow upon these two passages an authority sufficient to outweigh all those that could be quoted on the other side. To establish Christ-mysticism in its Jewish soil, he had only to shape his doctrine of righteousness through "being-in-Christ" as a new form of the "Scriptural" doctrine of righteousness by faith.

> For all who rely on works of the law are under a curse; for it is written, "Cursed be every one who does not abide by all things written in the book of the law, and do them." Now it is evident that no man is justified before God by the law; for "He who through faith is righteous shall live." . . . Is the law then against the promises of God? Certainly not; for if a law had been given which could make alive, then righteousness would indeed be by the law. But the scripture consigned all things to sin, that what was promised to faith in Jesus Christ might be given to those who believe. (Gal. 3:10–11, 21–22)

Here Paul bears his witness with all the passion of one who speaks autobiographically. He had been a Zealot of the Zealots on behalf of the law, but it had not brought him to righteousness. Indeed, he knew what it was inwardly to experience sin precisely through the law. The grace of God is to be understood as having put an end to the rule of the law through the death of Christ. It is the forgiveness of sins that is obtained by this death that brings about the redemption for the elect. And this forgiveness of sins takes place in the believer as the believer dies and rises again with Christ. It is unique with Paul in the early church that the death of Christ does not accomplish the forgiveness of sins automatically. The mystical identification with Christ in his dying and rising, as an interior death to sin and rising to newness of life in the believer—this too is required. It is the mysticism of Paul that has brought him to this distinctive position.

PAUL'S POSITION ON THE SACRAMENTS

It has often been held that Paul's position on the sacraments was derived from the mystery religions and was therefore Hellenistic. But, once again, we are to understand his emphasis upon the sacraments as motivated by his eschatology. The eschatological expectation of Judaism required that it become a religion of redemption and this in turn gave birth to the sacramental. As men project their eschatology of hope into the future, there comes the psychological need for some present assurance of personal salvation in the approaching day of Judgment. Baptism offers the sacrament of that assurance. John the Baptist finds at hand, in the prophets, justification for the ceremony:

> I will sprinkle clean water upon you, and you shall be clean from all your uncleannesses, and from all your idols I will cleanse you. A new heart I will give you, and a new spirit I will put within you. (Ezek. 36:25–26)

> Wash yourselves; make yourselves clean;
> remove the evil of your doings

> from before my eyes;
> cease to do evil.

> (Isa. 1:16)

> O Jerusalem, wash your heart from wickedness,
> that you may be saved.

> (Jer. 4:14)

The early Christian community appropriated this sacrament for its own without direct authentication by Jesus because its eschatology made the same demand that John the Baptist's eschatology had satisfied with the initiation of this act. In this sacramental act the promise of forgiveness for the faithful in the last days is reaffirmed as implicit in present repentance. The only change from the eschatological sacrament introduced by John is the notion of the immediate bestowal of the Spirit and that Jesus' name is evoked as well as God's and that of the Holy Spirit.

For Jesus, while he lived, baptism was unimportant because its benefits were secured by his very presence among the faithful and their fellowship with him. Even without their prior baptism, it was possible for Jesus to administer to them the sacrament of Holy Communion both in the feeding of the five thousand and at the last supper in thanksgiving for and in anticipation of the messianic feast to come.

The early church pursued the practice of a sacramental meal, not because of Jesus' saying about the bread and wine as his body and blood, but because it was understood as an exercise of petition and thanksgiving for the coming of the Kingdom. The characteristically Jewish meal of thanksgiving, familiar to the Jews at the time, had been transformed into an anticipatory celebration of the messianic feast, mystically experienced in the present. It is quite as much the sacrament of the return of the beloved Lord as the remembrance of his death on their behalf. So Paul's mystical genius leaves its indelible stamp on the church:

For I received from the Lord what I also delivered to you, that the Lord Jesus on the night when he was betrayed took bread, and when he had given thanks, he broke it, and said, "This is my body which is for you. Do this in remembrance of me." In the same way also the cup, after supper, saying, "This cup is the new covenant in my blood. Do this, as often as you drink it, in remembrance of me." For as often as you eat this bread and drink the cup, you proclaim the Lord's death until he comes. (I Cor. 11:23–26)

Both sacraments, for Paul, are inextricably related to his mystical conception of being-in-Christ. Through the dying and rising again, which begins in baptism, as he interprets it, believers cease to be attached to that natural existence in which they were separate from one another. Now they are neither Jews nor Greeks, men nor women, bond nor free, but partake together in a new form of humanity, a mystical communion in Christ. Henceforth they are called upon to walk, no longer in the flesh, but in the spirit, as befits men and women upon whom the resurrection mode has already been conferred. Moreover, the thanksgiving meal, which for Paul is a proclaiming of the death of the Lord "until he comes," is also a mystical act in which the eating and drinking both symbolize and effect present union in and with Christ. What makes the meal a sacred one for Paul is not the repetition of Jesus' words of institution; the real consecration is, rather, the inward act of thanksgiving and petition for the return of the risen Lord. Hence he who does not so participate desecrates the act, eats and drinks to himself death rather than life. Properly received, the act links all participants in a mystical communion one with another and with their Lord. Otherwise, it is merely a magical act. The being-in-Christ that was bestowed in baptism is maintained and nourished in the Lord's Supper, understood in this manner.

THE ETHICAL ELEMENT IN PAULINE MYSTICISM

One of the charges brought against mysticism is that in it the ethical element in religion is often lost. It will be well, therefore, to inquire briefly into the relationship of ethics to Pauline mysticism. For John the Baptist, for Jesus, and for the primitive Christian community, ethics is related to repentance. Insofar as conduct is ethical after baptism, this is the fruit of repentance. But for Paul, ethics is not a matter primarily of repentance. He does not even use the word when he is expounding his own ethical convictions. Repentance, it is true, is understood by Paul as involved in submitting oneself for baptism; but the whole of Paul's ethic is encompassed within the central notion of dying and rising again with Christ, of being-in-Christ. Ethical conduct is not then the fruit of repentance, but is the work of the Spirit that was in Christ. The same Spirit produces a new mind and a new heart; the ethical transformation is therefore, in reality, the fruit of the Spirit.

Moreover, it is not justification by faith which brings about the ethical man; it is the indwelling Christ who produces in him the good works. Those who have died and risen again with Christ, in the inner being, have entered a super-earthly world not open to those who strive for law righteousness. Being inwardly liberated from the "natural" world, they are ready to embark upon the "supernatural" life. There has been a transformation of the will. The one who is "in Christ" has "crucified the flesh with its passions and desires" (Gal. 5:24) and is able now, indwelt by Christ, to "walk by the Spirit" (Gal. 5:25).

How does Paul evade the tendency of some forms of mysticism to experience the eternal as passivity instead of a moral imperative? It is true that, for Paul, being-in-Christ brings a large liberty:

> Now the Lord is the Spirit, and where the Spirit of the Lord is, there is freedom. (II Cor. 3:17)

But this freedom has bounds. It is not to be imposed upon. Wherever this newly bestowed freedom might give offense to others, it is willingly to be forgone.

> "All things are lawful for me," but not all things are helpful. (I Cor. 6:12)

> "All things are lawful," but not all things build up. Let no one seek his own good, but the good of his neighbor. (I Cor. 10:23-24)

Even though freedom releases the Christian from scruples of eating and drinking, the Christian is to honor the conscience of another. The new liberty is to remain the servant of the love that was in Christ. As one would expect in the considered statement

of faith in the Letter to the Romans, Paul places his mysticism
and his ethics side by side, inextricably interrelated. The ethical
springs precisely from the dying and rising again with Christ.

> Let not sin therefore reign in your mortal bodies, to make you obey
> their passions. Do not yield your members to sin as instruments of
> wickedness, but yield yourselves to God as men who have been
> brought from death to life, and your members to God as instru-
> ments of righteousness. (Rom. 6:12–13)

It is not that man who has been liberated from the law is
lawless; he has been placed under a still more exacting, if infinitely more liberating, law, the law of love:

> For you were called to freedom, brethren; only do not use your
> freedom as an opportunity for the flesh, but through love be servants
> of one another. For the whole law is fulfilled in one word, "You
> shall love your neighbor as yourself." (Gal. 5:13–14)

The great ethic of love, derived from mystical union with the
love of God in Christ Jesus, is interpreted in the lyric poem of
I Corinthians 13 which concludes with the admonition, "Make
love your aim" (I Cor. 14:1). This love is the only true *gnosis,*
or knowledge, by which and in which God and those who are
in Christ know one another. The love of Christ is the same as
the love of God, which is in Christ Jesus. It is not always clear
whether the love of God and the love of Christ spring from God
and Christ or are felt for them by the believer. In any case, it
is all one, because the love of God and of Christ in the believer
springs from and bears witness to the actual love of God and the
love of Christ. The ethic of Paul is in fact the ethic of Jesus. In
Jesus it is one of preparing the Kingdom of God by being other
than the world. In Paul this being other than the world is
mediated by the mystical dying and rising again with Christ and
by the possession of the Spirit. Possession of the Spirit is mani-
fested by the chief mark of the Spirit: love. It is the very flame
of this love that constitutes the warmth, the passion, the constraint for the ethical. Of Paul himself it may be said that he
was an effective evangelist not primarily because of his great
mind, nor his extraordinary power of articulation in preaching,

but because, through his mystical identification with Jesus the Christ, he had become a great lover of men. It was his love for them that broke down the barriers.

So in Paul the concept of mystical dying and rising with Christ in practice produces a living ethic. In him, ethics becomes life in the Spirit of Christ. Though Paul was altogether rooted in the earth as a good Jew, his aspirations are yet fixed on heaven. Paul never ceases to have the ring of reality as a human being, but because of his Christ-mysticism he attains a larger, higher, freer humanity. In him, what would be unacceptable conceit in another becomes acceptable: "Be imitators of me, as I am of Christ." We can accept this because we know he spoke the truth when he said, "Who is weak, and I am not weak? Who is made to fall, and I am not indignant?" He boasted not, save of his weakness. In the last analysis, it was because he suffered more than his contemporaries on behalf of Jesus the Christ that he could presume to lead others with such confidence into his presence.

MAKING THE FAITH CAPABLE OF HELLENIZATION

We have seen how the mysticism of Paul the apostle can only be interpreted as eschatologically inspired. Therefore it was not Hellenistic. Though it has been said that Paul was responsible for Hellenizing Christianity, Albert Schweitzer has shown conclusively that it is truer to say that he prepared the way for its Hellenization. In the mysticism of Paul, Christianity assumed a form in a transition period which was capable of being Hellenized. His concern for the Gentile world had motivated him so to plumb the depths of his own distinctively Jewish world view as to arrive at an essence transferrable for reinterpretation in terms of another world view.

The crucial question was one of survival for the new religion, which was already failing to hold its own as a sect within Judaism. As the eschatological hope of an earthly Kingdom was longer and longer deferred, could it find a new home in the Hellenistic world view with its deep longing for immortality and its preoccupation with the dichotomy between the material and the spiritual? The pre-Pauline Christian faith, which to some extent continued as a tandem alternative even while his view was transforming it, was entirely focused on the coming of the Kingdom in which the Messiah, Jesus, would rule as King by virtue of his atoning death and resurrection. These thought patterns were alien to the Hellenic mind. However, the aspiration toward some form of redemption haunted the Greek mind as well as the Jewish. The redemption, associated earlier only with the coming of an earthly Kingdom, was in Paul transformed through his Christ-mysticism into a hope the Greek mind could entertain—redemption through union with the living person of Jesus the Christ. Redemption was no longer a future event alone, produced for the elect of Israel by the atoning death of a messiah, but a present possibility through a currently experienced resurrection life into which a believer might enter here and now by dying and rising again with the Christ, a mystical being-in-Christ.

By setting forth a viable claim that those who died in Christ might enter into the Kingdom on the still expected return of Christ rather than having to wait for a general resurrection, Paul removed another barrier to Hellenic acceptance. When he further connected this new idea with the sacraments, the ground was laid for a new interpretation of the Lord's Supper as the means by which the resurrection unto eternal life is assured. Thus the way was opened by which others could understand the sacrament of the Lord's Supper in thoroughly Hellenistic fashion as *the* saving "mystery" and the medicine of immortality.

The bridge by which the new faith could enter and find new life within the context of another world view was the notion of mystical union with the Christ, intellectually defended by Paul and charismatically transmitted by the fervor of his own sustained experience. His great achievement was to think through the meaning of his personal experience in such depth and cogency that it could have universal appeal. He gave the Christ myth a new form in which mystical union with a heavenly figure became the one thing needful for a redeemed life. The eschatological world view of Paul is totally obsolete, viewed from a post-Darwinian twentieth-century world view. But the saving power of mystical union with a person, Jesus, or with the Christ in Jesus, has demonstrated its capacity for transference from one world view to another and from one age to another, long separated in time.

CHRIST-MYSTICISM VERSUS GOD-MYSTICISM

Albert Schweitzer suggests that we too "should claim the right to conceive the idea of union with Jesus on the lines of our own world-view, making it our sole concern to reach the depth of the truly living and spiritual truth."[32] But Schweitzer sees this as necessarily taking the form of a "Christ-mysticism," a " 'belonging together' with Christ as our Lord, grasped in thought and realized in experience."[33] He discounts the viability of a God-mysticism or the possibility of its resulting in anything but "a passive determination of man's being, an absorption into God, a sinking into the ocean of the Infinite,"[34] devoid of ethical motivation and the power to produce a Kingdom of God on earth. Granted, this has been true of some Western as well as Eastern forms of God-mysticism. Nevertheless, it is my conviction that some form of God-mysticism rather than traditional Christ-mysticism, inextricably associated with the Jesus of history, is the only way forward within our present world view and our peculiar responsibility for dialogue with other world religions, for which Christ-mysticism as commended by Paul is an insurmountable stumbling block.

One wants to inquire of Schweitzer concerning Jesus' own peculiar form of mysticism. There was already in him, by implication, an element of "Christ mysticism." Jesus encouraged entering into the Kingdom through fellowship with him. But what of his own personal experience? Was not his in the deepest sense a God-mysticism? He had no Christ figure with whom to find mystical union. He had before him a historically grounded image which the prophets had drawn of a Messiah with whom it would appear he identified in some measure in his own self-consciousness. If, however, one is not to think of him as God become man in the traditional sense, "Very God of Very God, begotten, not made, being of one substance with the Father by whom all things are made," but rather as fully man, wherein lay the secret of his own religious faith? Was it not in a mystical identification with the Jewish God whom he had come to call "Father" and a mystical understanding of the Kingdom of God as something which was both present and to come?

If Jesus was God become man, it is meaningless to speak of him as a God-mystic. But if he was a man in every sense, then the only meaningful way we can understand his own faith, it seems to me, is in terms of God-mysticism. Hence we have been at pains to understand the historical Jesus as a Jewish mystic. The course of God-mysticism is in one sense more audacious for a Jew than for any other, save perhaps for a member of Islam, because of the insistence upon transcendence as the central characteristic of God. To speak of the immanence of God within the context of Judaism is always to be vulnerable to the charge of blasphemy. Yet this is precisely the significance of the human life of Jesus of Nazareth as I see it. If not uttering the bold, epigrammatic claim of an Eckhart, "My me is God," in so many words, is not this the inwardness of his aspiration and growing experience in attentive listening and willed obedience?

There is another approach to that authentic form of mystical religion whose power was manifest in Paul the apostle. Instead of mystical union with the evolving Christ myth to which Paul calls us, we may choose to learn from Jesus, as from a human brother, the secret of the practice of his own God-mysticism. The union would then be, not with the historic figure, Jesus become Christ and elevated to the right hand of God, but with the selfsame Spirit with whom Jesus had found interior, personal identification in his practice of living in the Kingdom. In this way we become disciples of Jesus, not that we may learn to call him God incarnate, but that we may learn of him "the way, and the truth, and the life." There will come a time in this discipleship when the human, historic figure will say to us, "Henceforth I call you no longer servants but friends."

It remains a fair question to ask whether the Jesus of history really intended more than to teach us, through preaching and example, the way to enter into and to live in the Kingdom. In any case, it is my conviction that we are to learn from Jesus the nature of his own mystical experience, and to pursue its lead. Becoming thus more profoundly brothers of the firstborn, we need not repel our contemporary brothers in other faiths by addressing him as Lord and directing to him a reverence that belongs only to the imageless God. Schweitzer's conclusion would appear too dogmatic:

> In Jesus Christ, God is manifested as Will of Love. In union with Christ, union with God is realised in the only form attainable by us.[35]

Jesus himself had discovered the way inwardly in which to unite with that Father-God whom he had known as Will of Love. While the disciple is not above his master, when he has been addressed as friend need he be any less audacious? Paul was prevented "by his eschatological world-view from equating Christ-mysticism with God-mysticism." But we are not so bound. We may essay with the Nazarene a mysticism that can free us for deeper communion not only with contemporary Jews but with followers of the other living religions as well. If we but penetrate to the very heart of the experience that lies at the fountainhead of our own religion, we shall meet him who has not left himself without witness at any time or place on common ground with our brethren of other faiths. He is indeed the common ground of our shared "being." That this audacious pursuit will inevitably carry peculiar dangers we do not doubt. It is a narrow way, here, as always, that leads into life. Nevertheless, the peculiar demands of our age require that we explore this way forward.

THE KINGDOM OF GOD AND THE MEANS OF ENTRANCE

Immediate participation in a Kingdom of God as revealed most fully to us by Jesus remains the ever elusive object of our passionate quest for redemption. That this still requires an interior dying and rising again there can be no shadow of doubt for all who have begun to know and to acknowledge what is in man. But this dying and rising again need not be literally attached in the aspirant's imagination with Jesus' own death and resurrection in an obsolete eschatological context. As Paul put together in balance the two great elements of the primitive Christian faith, commitment to redemption into the Kingdom and the path to its realization through the mysticism of being-in-Christ, so we may retain the vision of the same distinctive Kingdom, understood as a present potential for those who will pursue the God-mysticism that was Jesus' own "way and truth and life." What "the patron saint of Christian thought" was able to achieve within the thought patterns of his own eschatological world view we must dare to undertake anew in our post-Darwinian and post-Freudian century. Once again, we would acknowledge with Schweitzer that in the mysticism of Paul the apostle we see united the idea of redemption through Christ and a living belief in the Kingdom of God on earth. This combination must also be part of any living faith in the future, though one must be allowed to interpret in new and universal terms redemption through the Christ way revealed in Jesus. So one of the greatest of the modern mystics, a spiritual God-child of Paul the apostle, lets us catch a glimpse of the core of his basic religious experience and commitment. But he himself counseled against "half-way history and half-way thought." Therefore for us the conception of "the redemption through Christ" must now become "thinkable and true" for our day.

I agree with Schweitzer's analysis of Christian history. It is precisely the failure of any subsequent generation to recover in like balance these two emphases that has prevented a comparable return of the fervor of the primitive church. Sometimes it has been the vision of the authentic Kingdom of God that has been lost sight of in the pursuit of personal salvation, as in Hellenized Christianity and that of certain periods of Catholicism and the Protestantism of the Reformers. Sometimes it has been the loss of the sense of mystical union with Christ (though we should prefer to say "with God") in vain pursuit of a Kingdom without interior personal transformation, as with certain social gospel actionist movements. The living unity and balance do need to be reestablished, that the church become neither sterile through quietism nor weary in well-doing because the spring of its true energy has been neglected.

It is Jesus himself who speaks to the condition of our day as much as to his own time with the words:

> Seek first his Kingdom and his righteousness, and all these things shall be yours as well. (Matt. 6:33)

That this Kingdom for those who would call themselves Christians is to be sought in Jesus' company and in his way, we have made clear. We turn therefore to one who is greater than Paul for counsel in fulfilling the primary responsibility which he has so brilliantly put before us. With our particular perspective of man in evolutionary context we have more justification in one way for belief in the possibility of an earthly Kingdom than any previous generation. We also have more reason to be attentive to the mystics as constituting, perhaps, the forerunners of the new race of men, man's successor. Paul's claim that Jesus was the firstborn of many brethren has strange new relevance in our twentieth-century mode of thought. Schweitzer makes final claim of the greatness of the apostle Paul:

> Paul is so great that his authority has no need to be imposed upon anyone. All honest, accurate, and living thought about Jesus inevitably finds in his its centre. . . . If the Gospel of Paul, the primal Christian mystic, strikes the keynote of our faith, the Gospel of Jesus will sound forth clear and true. . . . In the only possible logical way, Paul's thought transforms the ethic of Jesus into the ethic of the Kingdom of God which Jesus brought, and in doing so it retains all the directness and force of the ethic of the Sermon on the Mount.[36]

Certainly Schweitzer stood clearly within the apostolic succession of mystics and was himself one of the latter-day brethren of the firstborn. On his testimony it is clear that Paul more than any other person influenced both his passion for truth and the mystical quality of his personal faith. If both Paul and Schweitzer speak to us with authority, we shall in loyalty to their example assert the rights of thought in the Christianity of our day and chart a course for the mystical way that will be compatible with the world view appropriate to our time.

Chapter VII

The God-Mysticism of the Fourth Gospel

We have seen the extraordinary claims that Albert Schweitzer has made for the work and subsequent influence of Paul the apostle. No less extravagant praise has been given by others to the achievement of the author of the Fourth Gospel, who has traditionally borne the name of John. The succession of tributes goes back to the church fathers. Clement of Alexandria wrote as follows:

> Last of all, John, perceiving that the bodily [literal] facts had been set forth in the other gospels, at the instance of his disciples, and with the inspiration of the Spirit, composed a spiritual gospel.

Origen, commenting on the depth of its insight and wisdom, suggested that no one could fully understand it who had not, like John, lain upon the breast of Jesus. For Luther, this was "the chiefest of the Gospels." Drummond characterized this Gospel as possessing "tender and unearthly beauty." William Temple designated it "the profoundest of all writings." W. A. Smart has made the claim that "more people have gone to these few pages for strength and comfort in life's hard places, for deep and abiding faith, and for thrilling assurance of the presence of God in their lives, than to any other single writing ever penned." In another place he calls it the "greatest and most influential Christian writing of all time." Dean Inge accorded it the distinction of being "the charter of Christian mysticism."

It is impossible to assess the value of these statements. Certainly in the peculiar statement of the Gospel of Love by the author of this document a powerful influence has been released.

No other book in the New Testament has lent itself so often or so effectively to devotional use as this one. As we consider its message we shall see many of the characteristic elements of the mystical approach to religious experience to which we have already referred.

First we must explore a little further the way in which Paul's thought constituted a bridge from the Jewish (eschatological) to this Hellenistic form of mysticism. It will be well to remember that it is precisely the mystical element that can be held in common by differing interpretations of religious truth. Indeed, mysticism is the very language of communication between Christian theologies as well as between different faiths.

THE HELLENIZATION OF PAUL'S MYSTICISM BY IGNATIUS AND JOHN

We have seen that Paul did not Hellenize Christianity. He did in fact prepare it for Hellenization, and this by reason of his mysticism. The nonmystical, primitive Christian faith, not yet transformed by the Pauline mystical genius, was composed of certain elements incapable of Hellenization. These included the belief in the fast-approaching earthly Kingdom; the messiahship of Jesus as revealed in an atoning death and resurrection; and admission into this Kingdom through repentance and baptism. In this theological milieu the place of Jesus was dependent upon the notion of the Messiah who would swiftly usher in the anticipated Kingdom. When the expectation of the immanent Kingdom began to wane, the Christian faith survived because Paul had fashioned a concept of relationship to the person of Jesus the Christ independent of the impending eschatological fulfillment. The relationship that Paul first experienced and then interpreted was that of mystical union with Christ, a being-in-Christ. The idea of individual resurrection was associated with union with Christ as effect with cause. In his insistence that the "dead in Christ" will arise automatically at the return of Christ, Paul prepared the way for the later Hellenistic emphasis on immortality produced by union with Christ. For Paul, an inward participation in the sacraments through the mystical be-

ing-in-Christ qualified a person for life in the messianic Kingdom now, not merely for the general resurrection to eternal life
at the close of the age. Out of this Pauline innovation could
come the next stage of adaptation by Ignatius, who interpreted
the Lord's Supper as a food conferring immortality.

This subtle but important change took place even while the
return of Jesus and the coming of the Kingdom could still be
entertained as a plausible hope. Ignatius made allusion in his
Epistle to the Ephesians (ca. A.D. 110): "The last times have
come."[37] The Epistle of Barnabas (21:3) was still prophesying
with confidence: "Near is the day on which for the wicked all
is lost; near is the Lord and his reward." Meanwhile, the prayers
of thanksgiving used in the liturgy, as reported in the *Didache*
(chs. 9–10), expressed the fervent expectation of the Messiah's
return. The hope of the eschatological Kingdom could not of
itself appeal within the Hellenistic ethos, but a mystical union
with Christ, which could produce immortality, had coinage
value. Because Paul interpreted the resurrection of Jesus as itself
beginning a resurrection state which others might in some measure share by mystical union with him, a language of communication had been forged. Ignatius and other theologians in Asia
Minor were thus enabled to hear the mystical message that
could no longer be imparted solely in eschatological terms.
Ignatius and Polycarp do not use Paul's theological terminology
of dying and rising again with Christ. The new articulation of
the same mystical experience in language acceptable to the Hellenistic theological milieu describes union with Christ as producing a union of flesh with Spirit.

The subtle change lies just here: for Paul, the Spirit is bestowed upon the believer as a result of the dying and rising again
with Christ, whereas for these Hellenistic theologians the Spirit
is an inherent part of the natural man, however existentially
sundered from the flesh. The resurrection takes place within the
context of the already existing presence of the Spirit. The flesh
is not done away with or superseded, as in Paul, but transformed
through the Spirit at work within. For Ignatius and his contemporaries in Asia Minor the Pauline mysticism of being-in-Christ
is given the new interpretation of union of flesh and Spirit.

Hence the way is opened to the development of the idea of the union in Jesus of the divine and the human and the accompanying idea of the union of the Spirit and the flesh in the believer through mystical union with Christ in the sacraments.

Thus an internal shift of cardinal importance has occurred. The emphasis has moved from the death and resurrection of Jesus to the incarnation. In the light of current ideas about the nature of the psyche, it was the appearance of one on the earth in whom a unity of flesh and Spirit was manifest from birth that ultimately makes possible such interior union in the believers, and forms the basis of the possibility of the resurrection of the body and the life everlasting. There is also an accompanying shift in relative significance from the sacrament of Baptism to that of the Lord's Supper through which now the very process of redemption is mediated. The bread and the wine now symbolize the union in Christ of Spirit and flesh.

THE ROLE OF THE SPIRIT IN BAPTISM AND THE LORD'S SUPPER

Another important development is a modulation from the notion of "being-in-Christ" to the notion of "being-in-God." This is the first great unconscious effort to return from a religion about Jesus to the religion of Jesus—a being in God in terms acceptable to the Greek psychology. This is accomplished by relating the Greek notion of Logos to the preexistent Christ and to the historic Jesus who proceeds from the Logos. The being-in-Christ becomes a being-in-Logos or being-in-God. At this time the idea of a rebirth for the believer appears. It is an expression Paul does not use. It means reproducing in the believer what took place at birth in Jesus, namely, the union of Spirit and flesh. This rebirth takes place through water and the Spirit; that is to say, the formal sacrament of Baptism is not of itself sufficient. Baptism by the Spirit as well as by water is necessary for rebirth. The born-again believer must also be nourished in the life of the Spirit-flesh by eating and drinking the body and blood of the Son of Man. The Fourth Gospel represents Jesus as the real source of such teaching, since the authority for it cannot be found in Paul. Jesus alludes to what will take place after his departure, when the Spirit will come and not only lead men into all truth but also into redemption through its union with water in Baptism and with the elements in the Eucharist. The implication is clear in the discourses imputed to Jesus, that the sacraments and the Spirit are inseparable; where the sacraments are, there is the Spirit. During Jesus' earthly life the Spirit is confined to him; when he goes to be with the Father, the Spirit will come to be with the disciples. From our perspective we could say the same of the Christ: confined to Jesus while he lived, present in the disciples ever since.

> For as yet the Spirit had not been given, because Jesus was not yet glorified. (John 7:39)

> Nevertheless I tell you the truth: it is to your advantage that I go away, for if I do not go away, the Counselor will not come to you; but if I go, I will send him to you. (John 16:7)

Now it is precisely the Logos which came in Jesus that is to come again when he goes, this time as the Spirit. For this reason the being-in-Christ in the Johannine sense can take place only after the death of Jesus. So the being-in-him is connected with eating and drinking the flesh and blood of the Son of Man.

> He who eats my flesh and drinks my blood abides in me, and I in him. (John 6:56)

It is also related by Jesus to the coming of the Spirit in many allusions in chs. 14 through 17.

By the same token, until Jesus has gone and the Spirit has come, baptism can be by water only. It is for this reason that John is at pains to tell us that Jesus himself did not baptize and represents Jesus as pointing forward to that time when baptism can indeed be by the Spirit as well as by water. It is of baptismal water, fused with Spirit, to which Jesus refers in speaking to the Samaritan woman by the well. It is that water which he will give and which is capable of springing up as a well of living water even unto eternal life.

> Every one who drinks of this water will thirst again, but whoever
> drinks of the water that I shall give him [i.e., through the Spirit,
> after I am gone] will never thirst; the water that I shall give him will
> become in him a spring of water welling up to eternal life. (John
> 4:13–14)

Moreover, water plays a symbolic role in a number of the miracles that Jesus performs. He is able to change water into wine
at the wedding in Cana. The water in the pool at Bethesda is able
to heal when Jesus infuses it with Spirit. Jesus can walk upon
the water disturbed by the wind (Spirit) because he is himself
Logos-Spirit which it must perforce obey. Again, he heals the
man who has been blind from birth by putting spittle (water)
upon his eyes and commanding him to go hence to bathe them
in the pool of Siloam. All these miracles in a veiled way point
thus through the association between water and Spirit in the
deeds of Jesus to that union in Baptism possible after his departure. The final force of the argument is driven home by insisting
upon the truth of the report of the strange admixture of blood
and water that flowed from the spear wound upon his death.
Henceforth, John is suggesting that the Logos-Spirit which
came in Jesus and left with him is to return as Spirit and will
be henceforth present in the water of Baptism and the wine of
the Lord's Supper. The First Letter of John rehearses the mysterious relevance of this trinity: water, wine, and Spirit.

> Who is it that overcomes the world but he who believes that Jesus
> is the Son of God? This is he who came by water and blood, Jesus
> Christ, not with the water only but with the water and the blood.
> And the Spirit is the witness, because the Spirit is the truth. There
> are three witnesses, the Spirit, the water, and the blood; and these
> three agree. (I John 5:5–8)

Though the disciples baptize with water during the life of
Jesus, they cannot baptize with water and Spirit until his departure. To do so even then, however, they themselves must have
been baptized by water and by Spirit. Schweitzer thinks that this
is in fact the significance of the foot-washing incident which in
John takes the place of the Lord's Supper as the central sacrament at the last supper. Through water he ceremonially washes

and makes them clean. That they have thus been baptized by
water in this manner will only occur to them later. Had this
Baptism not taken place, though they were ignorant of its significance at the time, they would not later have been able to have
"a part in him" to the extent then of being able to baptize others
by Spirit as well as by water. So, when Peter protested inno-
cently, "Lord, do you wash my feet?" Jesus replied:

> "What I am doing you do not know now, but afterward you will
> understand." Peter said to him, "You shall never wash my feet."
> Jesus answered him, "If I do not wash you, you have no part in me."
> (John 13:7–8)

John's contention that Jesus did not otherwise baptize, nor
could Baptism be efficacious until after his death, is consistent
with the implied completion of the sacrament when, after the
resurrection of Jesus, he breathes the Holy Spirit into them.

> Jesus said to them again, "Peace be with you. As the Father has sent
> me, even so I send you." And when he had said this, he breathed
> on them, and said to them, "Receive the Holy Spirit." (John 20:
> 21–22)

Henceforth the disciples are capable of performing the sacrament in its consummate form. The framework for the church's
insistence on apostolic succession has been thus established
through the cornerstone of this conception. The completion of
the disciples' baptism by the infusion posthumously of the Spirit
by Christ himself bestows upon them the awesome authority
that has sometimes been so unscrupulously used.

> If you forgive the sins of any, they are forgiven; if you retain the sins
> of any, they are retained. (John 20:23)

For Paul, though Baptism necessarily had to wait until after the
death and resurrection of Jesus, since it involves the death and
resurrection of the believer through being-in-Christ as well,
there is no such fine distinction laid upon Baptism by water and
by Spirit. The logical sequence as sketched in the Fourth Gospel
has not yet been expounded.

John also draws similar analogies in the miracle of the feeding of the multitude at the lakeside. As in Baptism water would become the channel for the efficacious action of the Spirit, so Jesus demonstrates during his earthly ministry the way in which bread will become living when it becomes the channel for the Spirit's operation in the Eucharist. So the future significance of bread in the sacrament is prophesied in advance. As the water offered by the Samaritan woman is distinguished from the living water by which Jesus is nourished and which will later be present in Baptism, so the earthly bread offered to Jesus by the disciples, and rejected for the same reason, must be distinguished from the living bread resident in him and to come through the Spirit.

> Meanwhile the disciples besought him, saying, "Rabbi, eat." But he said to them, "I have food to eat of which you do not know." So the disciples said one to another, "Has any one brought him food?" Jesus said to them, "My food is to do the will of him who sent me, and to accomplish his work." (John 4:31–34)

He then indicates that the fields were ripe for harvest, alluding to that harvest unto eternal life which is yet to come. Even as the union of Spirit and water must await his death and resurrection, so must the union of bread and Spirit. His body will go to the earth as seed corn and the Spirit will spring up in its place. When he has gone to the Father, then will the disciples be able to harvest the bread of life and administer it in the Eucharist. As he speaks, the disciples would not grasp the full meaning of what he is saying. Never mind. There will be much time later for sustained reflection, and the Spirit himself will provide them the right understanding. Let them then ponder another word:

> The hour has come for the Son of man to be glorified. Truly, truly, I say to you, unless a grain of wheat falls into the earth and dies, it remains alone; but if it dies, it bears much fruit. (John 12:23–24)

THE INCARNATION SUPERSEDES THE DEATH AND RESURRECTION

Since in Ignatius and in the Fourth Gospel the incarnation assumes even greater significance than the death and resurrection, their importance (in distinction from the centrality which Paul accorded them) derives from making the extension of the incarnation possible through the sacraments. John's Hellenistic mysticism becomes a sacramental mysticism to a larger extent than was true even with Paul.

> So Jesus said to them, "Truly, truly, I say to you, unless you eat the flesh of the Son of man and drink his blood, you have no life in you; he who eats my flesh and drinks my blood has eternal life, and I will raise him up at the last day. For my flesh is food indeed, and my blood is drink indeed. He who eats my flesh and drinks my blood abides in me, and I in him. As the living Father sent me, and I live because of the Father, so he who eats me will live because of me. This is the bread which came down from heaven, not such as the fathers ate and died; he who eats this bread will live for ever." (John 6:53–58)

All this was quite inexplicable to the disciples at the time. In their bafflement they say, "This is a hard saying; who can listen to it?" (John 6:60). Again Jesus responds in a riddle that will be read fully when he is no longer with them, and indeed not adequately until the sacramental teaching has been fully developed by the church.

> But Jesus, knowing in himself that his disciples murmured at it, said to them, "Do you take offense at this? Then what if you were to see the Son of man ascending where he was before? It is the spirit that gives life, and the flesh is of no avail; the words I have spoken to you are spirit and life." (John 6:61–63)

What took place in the incarnation, namely, the original union of flesh and Spirit in the man Jesus, will have its continuing life in the union of flesh and Spirit in the believers, through the Spirit-filled and Spirit-conveying water in Baptism and bread and wine in the Eucharist. The Spirit, through the death and resurrection of Jesus, will be able to unite with the elements in the sacraments even as the Logos-Spirit had united with these basic elements—water, flesh, and blood—in the body of Jesus at his birth. But before this development can be realized, Jesus must die. Just as for John, Jesus could not have baptized even his disciples, save in that provisional and to-be-completed way at the foot washing, so the supper could not have taken place, for John, as reported by the Synoptists because the Spirit could join with the elements in the appropriate way only when Jesus himself was no longer there. So in one sense the disciples will be able to perform even greater works because, through the sacraments which they will dispense, the Spirit, whom Jesus will send, will give men life who in a deeper sense are dead until that moment.

> For the Father loves the Son, and shows him all that he himself is doing; and greater works than these will he show him, that you may marvel. For as the Father raises the dead and gives them life, so also the Son gives life to whom he will. (John 5:20–21)

As it was the indwelling of the Logos in Jesus that gave him divine as well as human life, so the return of the Logos in the Spirit, infused into the life of the believer through the sacraments, bestows immortality.

> While the eschatological framework was still with the church—for the hour is coming when all who are in tombs will hear his voice and come forth, those who have done good, to the resurrection of life, and those who have done evil, to the resurrection of judgment (John 5:28–29)—

the mysticism that Paul had implanted was capable of reinterpretation in a more universal language in the Hellenistic world. The sacraments could thus become both the means of and the expression for the mystical union, not only with Jesus the Christ but with the Logos in him or with God himself, and thus afford salvation through resurrection to eternal life. Almost unnoticed in the subtlety of its modulation into the new teaching acceptable to the Greek mind, Paul's noncorporeal resurrection had become a flesh and bones resurrection, and the eschatological Messiah had become the harbinger of immortality. By abandoning the Pauline idea of dying and rising again with Christ as the specific context for the mystical theology, and presenting itself in the simpler form of the redemptive work of the Logos-Spirit that was in Christ, the Hellenization has been achieved. From this point the Pauline mysticism is able to undergo other transformations in expression of content. We cannot agree with Schweitzer's lament that the Pauline mysticism is superior or possesses a warmer life than the Ignatian or the Johannine, because "it expresses the relation with Christ experienced by a great personality, whereas the Ignatian-Johannine is the outcome of a theory."[38] The charge that the ethical content of the Pauline mysticism was impoverished in the Hellenization does not seem defensible to me. Love is given a more metaphysical interpretation in John than in Paul, and the discourses of Jesus seem wanting in ethical force. But this may simply mean that the author assumes that conduct motivated by love will be ethical in content. If a man but love God with the love that was in Christ, he may well do as he pleases.

IDENTITY AND PURPOSES OF AUTHOR OF FOURTH GOSPEL

The identity of the author of the Fourth Gospel has never been resolved, nor is it likely that any new evidence will arise to make this possible. Ever since the latter half of the second century, the tradition initiated by Irenaeus, Clement of Alexandria, Tertullian, and the Muratorian Canon has attributed the authorship to John, the son of Zebedee. Most recent scholars, including E. C. Hoskyns, Rudolf Bultmann, C. H. Dodd, and C. K. Barrett, agree that the author, whoever he may have been, was a Palestinian Jew, as indicated by his familiarity with the geographic details and his intimate knowledge of Judaism. He was familiar with the records of Jesus' ministry, and some have felt that his chronology in certain specifics may actually be the more accurate. Certainly he was one who had come into close touch with rabbinical Judaism and with Hellenized Judaism as well as with Gnosticism. Some have thought that the elder John at Ephesus is the actual author but that John the apostle stands behind the gospel as the witness. Others feel that at least two different disciples of John are involved, accounting for differences between the first twenty chapters and the last chapter.

Both Charles Raven and William Temple came to the considered judgment either that the apostle John stands behind the writing as the witness or that in ripe old age he may indeed have been the actual author. Some have felt that the emphases within the Gospel could not have come from the son of Zebedee, even had he lived to the close of the century, because the very character of the man as portrayed in the Gospel seems incompatible with the spirit here reflected. Yet, if we allow for the possibility of a character transformation through contact with Jesus, we can make psychological sense of it. An unlovable young man, marked by overweening ambition and violent temper, could become in the end one who knew himself as "the beloved disciple." He would have willingly abandoned both ambition and violence in the name of that love he felt constrained to interpret as the heart of the Gospel. This was perhaps one of the greatest healing miracles performed by Jesus. The inflation of ambition is transformed into humility. The enacted parable of the foot washing at the last supper has not been wasted upon him. The one who wanted a favorite place in the forthcoming Kingdom is now content to be the servant of all. This "son of thunder" has had his violent temper along with his love of power transformed into meekness by the power of love. This disciple knew himself as "the beloved disciple." Reticence born of humility demands that he speak in veiled language, but witness he must!

The central purpose of the Gospel is clearly declared:

> That you may believe that Jesus is the Christ, the Son of God, and that believing you may have life in his name. (John 20:31)

It is true that there are at least three polemical concerns: to condemn the hostility of the Jews, to discredit the sect that claimed John the Baptist as its head, and to answer false claims of Gnosticism in its docetic form by marshaling arguments from its own arsenal against them. The way in which his points are made would seem now and again a violation of the spirit of love. It is not individuals who are condemned, however, but movements that are denying the truths he is trying to defend. The book is primarily one of personal testimony, that of a profound mystic who has happened on the highest reaches of human experience in fellowship with the divine. The general tone is not that of a debate but of an impassioned witness. To him the Gospel is life, light, and love.

John is telling us what Jesus the Christ means to him. Inevitably, at this distance in time from the transforming experience, he is representing Jesus as speaking to everyone as he has spoken to him. The literary style of the long discourses of Jesus is the same style in which the author writes when he is not attributing the words to Jesus. We are perhaps thirty years farther away from Jesus than we are in the Synoptics. Yet the personal recollections of one very close to him are involved, even if mediated by another. And recollections of experiences that have worked life transformation can be both vivid and abiding.

There is another consideration. It would take a mystic to understand the experience of a mystic and to interpret the inwardness of it. Though the words may be more John's than anything Jesus ever spoke, his psychological understanding of the Nazarene, his imaginative projection into his Lord's self-consciousness, his intuitive grasp of the nature of Jesus' own mystical experience, may be closer to the heart of what meant most to Jesus than anything contained in the Synoptic Gospels. Just as Paul spoke as one having authority, even though by later standards he may not even have been properly ordained, so this mystic, undoubtedly influenced by the Pauline mysticism, is able to speak with the authority that mystic insight affords.

It is interesting that there are no parables in this Gospel. What holds the author in thrall is not the stories Jesus told, but metaphors or allegories he used in speaking of himself. They may be metaphors invented by the genius of a disciple who knew himself beloved, rather than issuing from the voice of Jesus, and yet they may reflect, with an integrity and appropriateness surpassing visual and audio fact, the mystical experience of him whose words they purport to be. Jesus is not speaking in the Gospel of John of the Kingdom, save now and again in some of its inward aspects as realized eschatology. He is speaking of himself, of his relationship to God and to his disciples. We are boldly taken by this author into the immediacy of the religious experience of Jesus, as John conceives this to have been. This is how John saw the Lord he loved; these are the words that Lord spoke into the depth of this disciple's being. This Lord was to him food and drink for his hungering soul, he was light in a world of darkness, he was life in the presence of impending spiritual death. He was the way in a world in which one could so readily lose one's way. He was the truth when many lies were corrupting the souls of men. And he was the very vision of the glory of God, for all men to behold.

There is another striking element in the mysticism of this author that has come to light through the studies of several scholars in the last decade. Not only did Jewish eschatology and some strands in Greek philosophy converge in his mind, but his synthesis seems to have encompassed ideas strikingly like those of Mahayana Buddhism. The regular maritime trade route between India and Egypt may well have put in circulation in the Mediterranean world some of the Buddhist notions. J. Edgar Burns in *The Christian Buddhism of John* feels that in some respects the thought of John is closer to Mahayana Buddhism than either Judaic or Hellenistic categories. John's theology of God based on the experience of love is like that of the Buddhist experience of prajna, or perfect wisdom. This would account in part for the recognition of many missionaries that it is the Fourth Gospel rather than the Synoptics that speaks to the Oriental mind.

God is the love, the light, and the spirit operative in human life. Both Mahayana Buddhism and John declare that it is in an act of believing a "secret teaching," or *gnosis,* that enlightenment is experienced. "This is eternal life, that they know thee the only true God, and Jesus Christ whom thou hast sent." As in Buddhism he who exercises perfect wisdom is said to be born of perfect wisdom, that is, realizes enlightenment, so in John "whoever loves is born of God." As in Buddhism *practicing* wisdom is enlightenment, so *doing* the truth in love is salvation in John. Abiding in Jesus, being righteous, and being born of God are all the same thing. God is made present through the actions of men. Both the Mahayana Buddha in the "Lotus of True Law" and the Johannine Christ preach a universal salvation. And curiously in the interpretation of both there is a tension between universalism and exclusivism. No one comes to Nirvana but by Buddha as no one comes to the Father but by Christ. Another analogy is that as the Lotus "takes root and lives in the mud," so the emphasis in John is on the Word made *flesh*. Again, there is a striking similarity between the word of Jesus that whoever has done anything for one of the least of his brothers has done it for him and the word of the Buddha to the disciple who ministered to a brother suffering from dysentery: "Always remember that what you do for helpless folk I take as a kindness done to me."

Valerie E. Viereck in *The Lotus and the Word* still further substantiates these claims. She notes that the strong *bhakti,* or devotional emphasis, in the sutra the "Lotus of True Law" is comparable to the devotional emphasis of the author of the Fourth Gospel and the epistles attributed to the same author. As the Buddha has no beginning or end, so Jesus was preexistent and shall reign at God's right hand forever. As all who are faithful to the gnosis in Christianity become sons of God, so do the followers of perfect wisdom become Bodhisattvas. As the Bodhisattva comes to recognize the "eternal primeval nature of the Buddha," so the task of the true Christian is to realize God's eternal reality in Christ. For both, there is the crucial choice between believing and not believing, a matter indeed of *life* or *death*.

Whether these analogies can be attributed to cross-cultural exchanges as seems likely, at least in part, or to the curious synchronicity characteristic of the experience of participants in "the perennial philosophy," that these mystical strains in two of the living religions were on a convergent course is dramatically demonstrated.

THE MIRACLES AS METAPHORS

Characteristic of the mystic is the mental habit of perceiving connections between things, events, ideas, that may seem to others unrelated. This is why the mystic loves metaphors and allegories. This kind of language best serves to reflect the experience. The miracles are therefore seen by John as themselves allegories. He first magnifies the details to make them appear more miraculous. He is at pains to tell us that the blind man had been *born* without sight, that Jesus' walking upon the water took place *twenty-five or thirty furlongs* from the shore, lest it be assumed by anyone that he might be walking in the shallows. The motivation for the performance of the miracles would seem not to be compassion but that the beholder might see and believe, exactly the opposite from what is claimed in the Synoptics. There the miracles proceed from the faith of the one healed, or someone close to that person. Here the object is that the miracle may produce faith. When the water has been turned into wine, we are told that "his disciples believed in him" (John 2:11). When the nobleman had inquired into the hour of the healing of his son, we are informed that "he himself believed, and all his household" (John 4:53). Jesus himself is reported more than once as pointing to his own miracles as ground for responsive faith:

> For the works which the Father has granted me to accomplish, these very works which I am doing, bear me witness that the Father has sent me. (John 5:36)

Our author is not lacking in compassion, but the vital concern for him is to persuade all who will listen to him to believe that Jesus was indeed the Christ, the Son of the living God. Hence the miracles become signs or symbols. Their significance becomes sacramental: they are outward and visible signs of inward and spiritual truths. They are pointing beyond themselves to a higher truth. Indeed in some sense the miracles in John take the place of the parables in the Synoptics in that they appear to be performed, not so much to relieve human suffering as to impart spiritual truth, even as allegories. In the turning of water into wine, that water in the presence of Jesus comes to life with capacity to intoxicate with joy when contrasted with the lifelessness of water in Jewish ablutions. If Jesus could heal the paralytic by the pool of Bethesda, the thing to remember was that he could also heal the paralyzed soul, for the critical comment with which that incident is closed is:

> See, you are well! Sin no more, that nothing worse befall you. (John 5:14)

When the man born blind has been made to see, the cryptic message with which Jesus accompanies the healing is:

> For judgment I came into this world, that those who do not see may see, and that those who see may become blind. (John 9:39)

The allegory is clear. Jesus is speaking of spiritual blindness.

One would have thought that a miracle so great as the raising of Lazarus from the dead would have found its way into the other Gospels. Whatever the reason that it did not, our author, having made the miracle appear as miraculous as possible, is finally interested primarily in the analogy to spiritual death and resurrection. Even as Martha chides him for coming too late to save her brother, Jesus further postpones bringing him back to life in order to make clear the allegorical import of what he is about to do.

> Jesus said to her, "I am the resurrection and the life; he who believes in me, though he die, yet shall he live, and whoever lives and believes in me shall never die." (John 11:25–26)

INTERPRETING THE DOCTRINE OF THE ESCHATOLOGICAL KINGDOM AS METAPHOR

We see John in the process of reinterpreting a dogma in a metaphorical sense that has been taken for the most part in a literal sense. All mystics have this inclination. Since what fascinates is the inwardness of things, they instinctively engage in what Teilhard has called the process of interiorization. So John begins the process of allegorizing the anticipated second coming, stressing the doctrine's metaphorical meaning. It is not that John has altogether abandoned the hope of Jesus' physical return to inaugurate the Kingdom. He occasionally speaks somewhat laconically of this expectation:

> For the hour is coming when all who are in the tombs will hear his voice and come forth, those who have done good, to the resurrection of life, and those who have done evil, to the resurrection of judgment. (John 5:28–29)

Lip service must be paid to a hope that has not altogether passed from the current scene. But his whole tendency is to take this dogma of belief and allegorize it just as he has done in the case of the miracles. He is more interested in the spiritual significance of that doctrine than its literal fulfillment. He transposes the future event into present realization. One of the crucial aspects of the mystical experience is the recognition of the eternal in the present moment. Hence what was understood to be a breaking in of eternity upon the passage of time must be capable of being telescoped into the present moment for the eyes of faith. What is to happen at the end of the times is reinterpreted as happening now, in this moment, within the context of mystical religious experience.

The apocalyptic hope was to see Jesus return as Messiah, trailing clouds of glory. For John this is part of the present affirmation, emerging out of the mystical experience of being-in-God with Jesus while he lived, and sustained through participation in the sacrament of the Lord's Supper.

> We have beheld his glory, glory as of the only Son from the Father. (John 1:14)

This glory had to be spiritually discerned. Not everyone could see it. But the heart of the message of our author at this point is that there is no real need for a second coming, for he had in fact come as Messiah at his first coming. Those who had truly seen Jesus had in fact seen not only the Messiah but the Father himself. The only sense in which it was necessary for him who came initially as Messiah to return again was as the Spirit, and as Spirit the second coming has already taken place.

> A little while, and you will see me no more; again a little while, and you will see me. . . . So you have sorrow now, but I will see you again and your hearts will rejoice, and no one will take your joy from you. (John 16:16, 22)

Christ has already returned in the Spirit and in the Spirit he will abide with his disciples forever.

The same practice of reinterpreting metaphorically what had been generally taken literally applies to the resurrection. He does not deny that a final day of resurrection will indeed come, but the significance of that day is as a continuing symbol of what in the realm of the Spirit is happening right now for those who have been dead in sin but are raised to new life in Christ Jesus.

> Truly, truly, I say to you, he who hears my word and believes him who sent me, has eternal life; he does not come into judgment, but has passed from death to life. Truly, truly, I say to you, the hour is coming, and now is, when the dead will hear the voice of the Son of God, and those who hear will live. (John 5:24–25)

The curious modulation from future event to present internal reality takes place in understanding a doctrinal statement as a metaphor of immediate interior experience. Only the words "and now is" in verse 25 mark the radical change in perspective of which the mystic alone is capable. By the same token, Jesus may proclaim in this Gospel, "I am the resurrection and the life" while his earthly life is yet in progress. And in this foreshortening of time into the eternity conveyed in the present moment, judgment too becomes a realized fact. The dread future assize is present condemnation for the unbeliever.

> And this is the judgment, that the light has come into the world, and men loved darkness rather than light, because their deeds were evil. (John 3:19)

Even eternal life, which had been described as to be bestowed at the end of the messianic reign, is to be presently appropriated by the believer. "This is eternal life, that they know [in present experience] thee the only true God, and Jesus Christ whom thou hast sent."

THE SACRAMENTS AS ALLEGORY

This same practice of allegorizing is applied to the sacraments. John, though a sacramentarian, is constrained to have us distinguish between means and end, the symbol and that which is symbolized. We are always in danger of participating in sacraments as if they had magical capacity to convey benefits. John insists that they be mystically understood and interpreted.

Hence in the Nicodemus story, Baptism is treated symbolically, and the story of the feeding of the multitude is told in such a way that its symbolic meaning as a sacramental meal may not be missed. The telling word is:

> I am the living bread which came down from heaven; if any one eats of this bread, he will live for ever; and the bread which I shall give for the life of the world is my flesh. (John 6:51)

The incident, as with the miracles, has simply become the text for a sermon, in this case on the Holy Communion, and the spirit in which one is to participate in it. One can imagine oneself actually present at an early form of the liturgy (John tells us these words were spoken in the synagogue) when these sentences follow:

> So Jesus said to them, "Truly, truly, I say to you, unless you eat the flesh of the Son of man and drink his blood, you have no life in you; he who eats my flesh and drinks my blood has eternal life, and I will raise him up at the last day. For my flesh is food indeed, and my blood is drink indeed. He who eats my flesh and drinks my blood abides in me, and I in him. As the living Father sent me, and I live because of the Father, so he who eats me will live because of me. This is the bread which came down from heaven, not such as the fathers ate and died; he who eats this bread will live for ever." (John 6:53–58)

THE SELF-CONSCIOUSNESS OF JESUS

We have now to consider the degree to which the author of the Fourth Gospel, partly through his own mystical capacity, penetrated something of the self-consciousness of Jesus. We may indeed find it impossible to credit Jesus with reflection upon the implications for himself of being the Logos incarnate as well as the Messiah. Such speculation would be irrelevant, since it would be based on an anachronism. Therefore words attributed to Jesus in a portrait based upon this assumption would strike us initially as historically unsound and therefore incredible. But the moment one allows that the man Jesus was possessed in superlative degree with the same faculty that many men and women of varying cultures and religions have experienced, namely, the mystical consciousness, then many of these same words assume a new significance and become quite plausible in their general import.

It is not that the historical Jesus thought of himself as the Logos or as God incarnate. It is rather that he knew himself to be in such close interior communion with the God he habitually called "Father," and so profoundly identified with the spirit and the will of that Father-God, that he was not sure how to distinguish between God's will and his own. He knew himself to be one with God. Despite all the assumptions and the teaching of his Jewish faith, insisting on the absolute transcendence of God, here, in his own immediate, existential experience, as he looked into the nature of his own self-consciousness in prayer and in his own peculiar practice of the presence, there was this dimension of immanence.

To what extent this related to his interior questioning of the possibility of being or becoming the Messiah, the Anointed One, we shall never know. We cannot altogether disentangle what was read back into the man Jesus by the early church in its conviction that he was to return as Messiah. Most scholars would allow the likelihood that he came to identify with, in the sense of lending support to, the Daniel conception of Messiah as Son of Man and with the vision of the suffering servant in the fifty-third chapter of Isaiah. What we are asking primarily is this: What is the nature of that special relationship to God in his own interior life, hid as it was with God from even those closest to him, which could embolden him to entertain the ideas that he must have known would be considered blasphemous?

Is not the only conceivable answer, humanly speaking, to be found in the mystical consciousness of the man Jesus in terms of what we have come to know of the nature of such consciousness through the autobiographical statement of other mystics? If we accept the premise that there does exist a "perennial philosophy," universal in extent, then the basic experience we are pointing to in Jesus, which must lie behind, beyond, and beneath any Messiah consciousness, must be understood in this light. If he was fully man, and we have adopted this premise as the only acceptable one for us today and our new perspectives of biological space-time and depth psychology, then we can claim for Jesus only a human faculty, however superlatively developed. Once again, if Meister Eckhart could exclaim with a confidence and a passion sufficient to produce his posthumous excommunication by the church, "My me is God," is it unreasonable to assume that something not altogether unlike this might have been possible in the self-consciousness of Jesus?

The mysticism of Paul the apostle, we have held, was predominantly a Christ-mysticism, expressed in the being-in-Christ terminology. The identification with the risen Lord, now in some sense also resident in the disciple, took so intense and poignant a form that Paul did not find it blasphemous to say: "I, yet not I, but Christ in me." We are suggesting that Jesus must often have felt much the same with regard to God: "I, yet not I, but God in me." Does he not indeed say as much in effect now and again, at least in John's portrait? When the source of his extraordinary capacity for healing is called into question, as in the instance of the man who had suffered a malady for thirty-eight years, John portrays Jesus as saying:

> Truly, truly, I say to you, the Son can do nothing of his own accord, but only what he sees the Father doing; for whatever he does, that the Son does likewise. For the Father loves the Son, and shows him all that he himself is doing; and greater works than these will he show him, that you may marvel. (John 5:19–20)

This can be read solely as the projection upon Jesus by the pious imagination of one for whom he had become Logos incarnate. But purely on the human level, though it may be difficult to imagine him expressing himself as a Jew before the assembled throng in this manner, that such thoughts were going through the mind of the healer is not only plausible but even probable and psychologically well-nigh necessary.

John has Jesus appeal to his works as evidence of his own mystical identification with God.

> If I am not doing the works of my Father, then do not believe me; but if I do them, even though you do not believe me, believe the

works, that you may know and understand that the Father is in me
and I am in the Father. (John 10:37–38)

Again, the teachings come from the Father, as well as the power
to perform the works. Not only do these arise within the mystical identification of the Rabbi with the Father, but there is the
implication that the hearer must test them by the touchstone of
his own mystical capacity, cultivated in obedience.

My teaching is not mine, but his who sent me; if any man's will is
to do his will, he shall know whether the teaching is from God or
whether I am speaking on my own authority. (John 7:16–17)

The corollary of failure in a man's mystical capacity through
disobedience is elsewhere alluded to:

You know neither me nor my Father; if you knew me, you would
know my Father also. (John 8:19)

As this Gospel moves forward to its inevitable climax, the
claims of Jesus grow ever more exalted and comprehensive. On
contemporary Jewish ears they must have fallen with the unmistakable ring of blasphemy if they were spoken as related by
John. If they were spoken by a person living in our twentieth
century with literal implication, they would be understood as
emanating from someone suffering some form of paranoia. Only
on the assumption that they are spoken with utter spontaneity,
almost naively, by one who emerges as the supreme mystic are
they acceptable. It should be remembered, moreover, that the
mystical identification is not only with the Father-God but with
the Kingdom of which Jesus patently believed he was the supreme interpreter.

I am the way, and the truth, and the life; no one comes to the Father,
but by me. (John 14:6)

Here Jesus is speaking of the Kingdom in which he knows
himself to have taken up citizenship, and which has become
more real to him than the kingdom of this world. But this
Kingdom is not his possession alone, as with the paranoid. It is
within and among all those who will pursue the same way, truth,
and life. And then, in response to Philip's query, "Lord, show

us the Father, and we shall be satisfied" (John 14:8), came the
ringing words, themselves in the light of contemporary Jewish
thought the ultimate blasphemy, and ample cause for execution:

> Have I been with you so long, and yet you do not know me, Philip?
> He who has seen me has seen the Father. (John 14:9)

If we were not so familiar with these words, the enormity of
the claim expressed in them would strike us with the power of
what in drama is called "the illusion of the first time." If we were
to hear them uttered by a contemporary, they would identify the
speaker as utterly mad. Once again what is required for understanding is the assumption that they arise within the context of
the mystical consciousness. It is as if Jesus were actually saying,
"Anyone who has seen me as I have seen myself in those moments when I have been unshakably aware of the interior identification of my mind and will with the mind and will of my
Father will have seen the Father in me." It is my conviction that
he would also have been quite ready to concede: "And whoever
has known himself united to the Father inwardly in obedience
has also seen the Father in himself."

Moreover, the mystical identification between the believer
and God is to be supported by that between the Master and his
disciples.

> Abide in me, and I in you. As the branch cannot bear fruit by itself,
> unless it abides in the vine, neither can you, unless you abide in me.
> I am the vine, you are the branches. He who abides in me, and I
> in him, he it is that bears much fruit. (John 15:4–5)

The great intercessory prayer in John, ch. 17, extends the
identification to one another, binding disciples, Master, and
God inseparably to one another.

> I am praying for them; I am not praying for the world but for those
> whom thou hast given me, for they are thine; all mine are thine, and
> thine are mine, and I am glorified in them. . . . I do not pray for
> these only, but also for those who believe in me through their word,
> that they may all be one; even as thou, Father, art in me, and I in
> thee, that they also may be in us, so that the world may believe that
> thou hast sent me. The glory which thou hast given me I have given

to them, that they may be one even as we are one, I in them and thou in me, that they may become perfectly one, so that the world may know that thou hast sent me and hast loved them even as thou hast loved me . . . that the love with which thou hast loved me may be in them, and I in them. (John 17:9–10, 20–23, 26)

We must therefore conclude that the author of the Fourth Gospel is a mystic, and it is precisely this fact which has enabled him to respond to and to interpret so effectively the Jewish mystic, Jesus of Nazareth. Such an understanding enables us to make psychological sense of what would otherwise be totally irrelevant and unacceptable to us in our own day. It is to this Gospel that we must go primarily for a portrait of Jesus "to the life" in that all-important aspect of his person as a mystic. If we are to be disciples of the same Master, we must learn from him the practice of God-mysticism. John is the great interpreter.

Chapter VIII

The Aesthetic Mysticism of Augustine

What would the church now be like had it elected to follow the approach to religious experience of Augustine in preference to that of Thomas Aquinas? We must concede at once the point which Lawrence Lowell of Harvard was fond of making: "Hypothetics is the most futile of all sciences." He would invariably follow this dictum with the query, "If you had a brother, would he like cheese?" Our question cannot really be answered. But it is important to see that the church is largely what it is in temper and disposition because this crucial decision was made. The issue was never put before a particular council and determined by vote. Events and influences simply gravitated toward the Thomistic way. In so doing, the major trend in philosophical undergirding for Christian theology became Aristotelian. It is fair to point out that it might have gone the other way. By following Augustinian thought it might have become Platonic in tone and quality. In accepting Aquinas as its mentor, the rational prevailed over the mystical.

The ecclesiastical succession of authority was vested in the Thomistic approach. The true apostolic succession, as this book maintains, remained one of mysticism. On the other hand, creedal statement and theological rationalism, given unexamined presuppositions, became the pattern of the accepted tradition and the philosophy of religious education. The less formalized contagion of mystical experience and doctrine was relegated to the monasteries, the status-less, the marginal, and the underground, and was always under suspicion when it surfaced or extended its influence too widely. Nevertheless, even in the organized church, despite the general mistrust of the establishment, mysticism proved to be a hardy perennial. No segment of the church was without its authentic mystics, whether it vested authority in the hierarchy or in the Bible, or emphasized liturgical practice or the ministry of the Word. However, they rarely rose to positions of either prominence or power. One might suggest that Augustine was the last of the great prelates whose dominant characteristic was the peculiar genius of the authentic mystic. While great mystics were to continue to become leaders in monastic orders, one would be hard put to find many of them among the bishops of the church after Augustine.

Augustine the African

In the apostolic succession of Christian mysticism, Augustine has occupied a unique place on a number of grounds. The biography of Augustine by one of his ardent admirers in the twentieth century, Giovanni Papini, makes use of understandable hyperbole. Nevertheless, its claims do not seem excessive.

"Just as ancient Egypt appeased her hunger with the corn of Egypt and Libya, so throughout ten centuries of the middle ages did the whole of Christianity feed upon the thoughts that had emanated from the fertile, lucid, and generous brain of an African from Tagaste."[39] If the hierarchy became more wary of its mystics during this period, many of the common people continued to hear them gladly.

In a day when the indigenous people of Africa are coming into their own, after being referred to for centuries as the inhabitants of the dark continent, it is appropriate to remember this matchless contribution to the whole of Western civilization by a native son of Africa. Augustine was a Numidian who spoke the Punic language, though from a child he must have been bilingual, his other tongue being Latin. Again, Papini reminds us of the inherent romance in the rising of this mystic from the soil of Africa:

As ardent as the sun of his native land, sensual and passionate like all of his race, his thought and writings rich in *vigor igneus,* Augustine is the greatest of all Africans. Although he wrote in the language of Virgil and was guided by Platonic thought until the Hebrew Paul threw open to him the realms of light, in certain characteristics he remained an African to the end of his days.

The instruments, moreover, that gradually led him to salvation were destined to come to Augustine the African out of Africa. Apuleius the Numidian first inspired him with a taste for Platonic mysticism; Platonius the Egyptian revealed God to him as a pure spirit; the example of Victorinus the African strengthened his desire to give himself up to Christ, and another African, Pontitianus, by acquainting him with the heroic life of Anthony of Egypt, drove him, still reluctant, to the baptismal font.[40]

THE CONFLICT BETWEEN THE SENSUOUS AND THE SPIRITUAL

From his very birth in A.D. 354, Augustine inherited from his parents almost irreconcilable characteristics: the sensuality of his father and the spirituality of his mother. At the age of seventeen he took a mistress, who later bore him a son, Adeodatus. One has the impression from the evidence that this good woman dearly loved him and was loyal to him all the years he continued to live with her, though his own unbridled sensuality led to promiscuity. All the while another part of his nature continued to aspire. One thinks of Teilhard's proverb, *"Tout ce qui monte converge"* ("Everything that rises converges"). This undiscourageable habit of reaching up, despite his earthbound proclivities, was destined to put him in contact increasingly with the best that his intellectual and spiritual environment afforded. But first, out of the intensity of his own interior dichotomy, he was drawn to Manichaeism, which seemed in its philosophy of dualism to reflect his own interior experience of unending war between good and evil, light and darkness. If he could project the blame upon an evil power, he could by so much reduce the burden of guilt. But there was something in him that would not be squelched, some clamoring for a nobler, holier life that Manichaeism did not satisfy. While the prayers of his devoted mother relentlessly importuned the eternal Judge, the Hound of Heaven pursued him

within his own breast. He describes for us the intensity of his
interior struggle.

> What delighted me more than to love and be loved? But I over-
> stepped those bounds that separate one soul from another and
> within which the light of chaste friendship shines brightly. Rather
> did the loathsome concupiscence of the flesh and my state of
> seething puberty envelop and blind my spirit with vapours that
> prevented me from distinguishing between serene affection and
> black lasciviousness, both of which flamed within me, forcing me,
> in my youth and weakness, into the abyss of lustfulness and plung-
> ing me up to the neck in sin.[41]

Augustine found himself in the condition that afflicted Paul.
The good that he would he did not, and the evil that he would
not, that he did. It is one of the central convictions of this book
that the mystic is very often one in whom there has raged a
conflict more intense than afflicts the average person and for
whom some reconciling principle, transforming image, or inte-
grating vision is the more urgent. The potential mystic is often
hag-ridden by incipient schizophrenia. Even as epilepsy would
appear to be a built-in physical shock therapy for restoring
temporary balance to one who might otherwise suffer schizophrenia, so mysticism sometimes appears a merciful spiritual
poultice to allay the fever of interior conflict. Paul found in the
love of Christ, first encountered incarnate in the disciple Stephen, a new law superseding the law to whose minutiae he had
tried in vain to be obedient. If the author of the Fourth Gospel
be John the apostle, he had found in the love of Christ the
unifying force that could bring to humility one consumed with
ambition and to gentleness of spirit one possessed of a violent
temper.

RESOLUTION THROUGH THE QUEST FOR BEAUTY

What was it in Augustine that subdued the strife which raged
within him and brought him at length the tranquillity of a
disciplined life? "Our heart is restless until it cometh to repose
in Thee." He had a fine mind, developed by good tutoring, that

equipped him to be an avid seeker for truth among the intellectuals who were his predecessors as well as his contemporaries. He was an incurable romantic despite the disciplines of philosophy and theology in which he was well versed, and the romantic is ever in search of a superior love, even as the thinker is driven to pursue superior ideas. But I would suggest that the characteristic in Augustine which enabled him in the end to find what constituted for him the touchstone of reality, the *coincidentia oppositorum* ("coincidence of opposites"), the unifying power, was perception of beauty.

In my judgment, great as was the thinker in Augustine, the philosopher and theologian, passionate as was the lover who found in the end embracement of his inner being by the Holy Spirit "sweeter far than embracement by the limbs of woman," the ultimate charisma that wielded the power in him to make him whole and to draw us to wholeness sprang from Augustine the aesthete, Augustine the artist. The transforming image, the miraculous power for the interior one-ing is revealed to us in the single line in the *Confessions:* "O Beauty, so old and so new, too late have I loved Thee!"

Everything that rises converges. The talent in Augustine that kept rising until it converged with mysticism was the capacity to behold and to respond to ever greater beauty. It may have begun with aesthetic response to the limited beauty of fine rhetoric. Later he abandoned rhetoric for its own sake in favor of the moral beauty that Apuleius revealed to him in a form of Platonic mysticism, confirmed by Cicero in *Hortensius* as disinterested contemplation. Still later he was drawn to the portrayal of God as pure spirit in the writings of Platonius. Then he perceived the beauty that was in Jesus through the witness of Victorinus, and the incomparable beauty of the same royal way of the holy cross in the heroic life of a fellow African, Anthony of Egypt. Concurrently, in ever reaching upward, he moved from fascination with the fleeting beauty of sexual attraction to the more abiding charm of a platonic friendship (to which he referred as "the sweetest my life has known") to the never palling beauty of the Holy Spirit at the depths of his own being and at the mysterious core of all humanity.

If one's severest temptation always springs from the perversion of one's greatest talent, as we have noted before, one's salvation finally lies in the complete commitment of this talent to the highest that can be known and experienced. For Augustine, the crucial talent was the perception of beauty. Happily for him, falling in love with the greatest beauty, which was and is the mystic vision, was not too late. It is a question whether it can ever be too late, provided it is thoroughgoing. For Augustine it came when he was still comparatively young, in his early thirties.

THE REORDERING OF PASSION THROUGH CONVERSION

When such a pulling together of disparate elements in the inner being takes place, no characteristic is lost. All are reordered in a new unity and integrity. No doubt William James is right about "the expulsive power of a new affection." What is expelled, however, are old affections and attachments, not the passionate nature from which they sprang. When Augustine's heart was won to the beauty that was in Jesus and his life-style, the elements in his nature were all brought together in a harmonious pattern, as iron filings spring into a new and ordered design when a magnet is held beneath the paper on which they rest. The ardor and passion that marked Augustine were simply given new direction. Conversion, for him, was not some routine conformity, as it often is, but a radical reorientation of mind and passion.

> In him—and herein we see a sign of coming greatness—the metaphysical processes were neither the calm ruminations of the philosopher nor the superficial dallyings of the indifferent dilettante. Augustine cast himself bodily into the furnace of thought; whatever he touched, even the coldest theories, immediately glowed with heat; he meditated not only with his brain, but with his heart, his very entrails, with all the powers of his spirit; his whole being was engaged in searching, and he suffered and rejoiced in his philosophical victories and defeats as if it were a question not of ideas, but of destiny, of life itself. As in love and friendship he was all ardour, so in his peregrinations in pursuit of truth he became a very flame.

So passionate was Augustine in his hunger that he deserved to have it satisfied at last by Christ Himself.[42]

Augustine's Gethsemane took the form of a demand that he abandon once and for all the carnal satisfaction of his passions. "The battle that raged in Augustine's breast was not between truth and error, God and Satan, faith and doubt, but between chastity and lust, the desire for perfect purity and the longing for sensual ecstacy, between the spirit and [carnal] sex." The example of Anthony's renunciation as told to him by Pontitianus had been the agent of the Lord that had exacted a like renunciation. Modern depth psychology would not fail to take note that it was the voice of an unseen child that directed him to the Scriptural passage he was to receive as a direct command from on high. As he wrestled with his conscience in the garden, "How long, O Lord, how long shall thy wrath endure against me? . . . When shall I achieve salvation? When cast off my fetters? Tomorrow, perhaps? Or the day after? Shall I always say tomorrow, and will today never dawn for me? Why not this very hour? Why not end it at once, now and forever?" then there came the voice of the child, ever the symbol of rebirth and the new life: "Take up and read, take up and read." Taking up the epistles of Paul, which had already won his intellectual assent, he opened them at random, and found that the first words upon which his eyes fell spoke to his condition, even as in the experience of Anthony. "Not in rioting and drunkenness, not in chambering and wantonness, not in strife and envying: but put ye on the Lord Jesus Christ, and make not provision for the flesh." (Rom. 13:13–14.) He received the words as the Word of God and forthwith pledged his obedience. What had won an earlier intellectual assent, following the perception of supreme beauty, was now confirmed by a movement of the will.

THE TWO WOMEN IN AUGUSTINE'S LIFE

In this dramatic redirection of his energies and commitments one wishes that Augustine had been able to preserve one other vital continuity. Had he been able to consecrate in Christian marriage the relationship he had maintained with his beloved mistress for some fourteen years, he would speak now to our modern sensibilities with even more authority. This faithful companion through his journeys in quest of vocation and of truth, this mother of his only son, we have every reason to believe he loved dearly. We feel the poignancy of the separation and wonder what grounds could really have justified putting her away, with seeming unforgivable cruelty. Certainly it was not because he had fallen in love with another. The most plausible reason is in some ways the least acceptable—that he yielded to the importunity of his mother that he should contract a marriage with one who was of nobler birth and possessed of more ample dowry. Had he indeed been married to the child bride she chose for him with these preconditions in mind, the injustice and irony of such a union at the expense of one who had loved him faithfully might well have precluded the authority of his subsequent charisma. If one can forgive Augustine for abandoning his mistress as he assumed vocation and prominence, it would be on the grounds that he may have too far identified her with the shadow of lust in his own psyche to achieve with her the new life. At least he did not, after his final conversion, supplant her with another.

The perspective of modern psychiatry would of course raise an eyebrow with regard to the relationship between Augustine and his mother. All his life he seems to have adored her with more than common filial feeling. Perhaps choosing a mistress at seventeen was a necessary assertion of independence from his mother in pursuit of his own identity. It may be that after he became drawn to the Christian faith, he projected upon his mother the madonna image where it became in a measure fixated, so that he could never unite this image with the mistress image which society as well as his own interior experience imposed so irradicably upon the companion of his youth and the years before his conversion. It is likely that his relationship to his mother was more profound than he experienced with any other living person. At any rate, his *Confessions* reveal the account of a shared mystical experience (one of the rarest phenomena in the history of mysticism) and this with his mother. He had been speaking with Monica of the things that are eternal and reaching with her toward the perception of beauty and truth.

> And while we were thus conversing and yearning for that Wisdom, we did indeed touch it with the farthest-reaching fibres of our hearts; and then we sighed, and leaving those fairest fruits of the spirit suspended above us, we descended again to a consciousness of the sounds that were issuing from our mouths where words are formed and expire.[43]

We have earlier said, with Thomas Merton, that no father can achieve a mystical experience for his son, however much he might aspire on his behalf. Presumably the same limitation holds for mother and son. Yet here this mother and this son, now possessed of his own maturity in identity, are rapt in one contemplative ecstasy. There is nothing quite like it in all mystical literature. Not long afterward, Monica died. It may be that Augustine did not thereafter long for any union with woman that could not achieve this degree of spiritual oneness.

AUGUSTINE THE ARTIST

Ever the artist, Augustine's contemplation was more of beauty than of abstract truth. In the treatise *De Musica* he tells of his love for music and of his readiness to leave the oratory to yield himself wholly to the enchantment of the nightingale "that so sweetly doth lament." Augustine qualifies as the patron saint of all who experience in listening to music their only recognizable mystical involvement. Just because he is prepared to join them in interior identification with melody, they ought to accord him the privilege of speaking to their condition on other levels. The *Confessions* is indeed a soliloquy that is a kind of lament to God. It is also a troubadour's lyric sung in solitude to the eternal Listener, the eternal Lover. It is far more profoundly poetic than the verses of lesser poets though it is cast in prose. It is indeed a symphony in which there are infinite variations upon a single theme: the love of God. It is perhaps the only great autobiography addressed solely to God. At the same time, it is music intended for any other solitary individual who is prepared to march to the beat of the same Drummer. And many there are who have found themselves strangely warmed by that melody and drawn to march in that apostolic succession.

It sometimes happens that a visionary anticipates by a leap of insight a discovery that will not take place for more than a millennium. So it was with Augustine. Not only was he in some sense the first modern psychologist by reason of the ruthless penetration of his introspection, questioning fifteen hundred years before Freud the innocence of the child at its mother's breast, recognizing the repressive potential of guilt, and examining the processes of identification and projection. He also reveals himself a prophet in both senses by anticipating Darwin in his perception of the elements of both continuity and emergence in the process we now call evolution. In *De Quantitate Animae* he gives us his first outline of mysticism, sketching the development in man of forms of consciousness which he shares with vegetative life right up to the mystic way in a succession of ever ascending manifestations. There are seven levels of consciousness. Vivification is the name Augustine gives to the vegetative soul which even plants possess. The second is sensation, which we share with the animal kingdom. The third level is art, which includes man's distinctive endeavors from plowing fields to writing poetry. The fourth he names virtue, which is reserved for those who are inner-directed and put the care of the soul above that of fulfillment of the body. The fifth is gladness or peace of mind, which is the grace bestowed upon one who achieves sustained purity of life. The sixth is vision, which is the reward of those who through obedience are altogether released from bondage to the flesh. The seventh is the gift of unity with God in contemplation, the apex of mystical experience.

The artist, Augustine, is not only the musician and the poet. There is also in his thought an architectural grandeur reminiscent of the Byzantine age in which he wrote. *The City of God* is a prose epic whose sweep of concern and range of thought have rarely been surpassed. For the period in which it was written it is fairly cosmic in scope. As what had been called the eternal city began to crumble under the impact of the barbarian hordes, Augustine dreamed of another city which knew no rust and where thieves could not break through or steal. Once again, he speaks in a singular way to our modern age. We too are an urban civilization though agrarian cultures have intervened. A modern theologian writes of "The Secular City," commending its strengths. But we still have the need to lift our eyes to the sacred city whose lineaments Augustine so well discerned. History has almost infinitely expanded in our contemporary perspective and is now coextensive with evolution itself. But Augustine was the first to take the entire continuum of known history and to encompass it in the one drama of redemption. His was an integrative mind, even as his spirit comprehended undifferentiated unity.

Artist that he was, Augustine dealt with theological thought as a painter does with oils on canvas. He was mindful of composition, of balance, of proportion. If one grasped the element of truth in some extreme position, it had to be balanced by a statement expressing a compensating truth in the opposite extreme. As tensions that are somehow resolved add interest and power to a great painting, so a theologian who is also a literary artist presents antithetical truths resolved in great syntheses. Sometimes paradoxes must be left standing, unresolved save in human experience itself. The authentic mystic is wise enough to let them stand without attempting resolution. We have seen the same genius in Paul and in the author of the Fourth Gospel, though Augustine raises these contrapuntal concatenations to a higher intensity. With what supreme art Augustine deals with the concept of God's grace on the one hand and the free will of man on the other. Always there lurks the haunting music of unresolved contradiction: "When is free will freer than when it cannot serve sin?" "Love and do as you please."

Though he is one of the great literary artists of all times, Augustine's art reaches its consummation in his mystical genius. He perceived beauty primarily in goodness and especially in the love of God, revealed in grace. He who in his youth had been a sensuous and passionate lover, once he had fallen in abiding love with the Holy Spirit, became the great interpreter of the love of God. Ever addressing God, he wrote, "At times Thou dost bring me to a state of strange and sweet plenitude of I know not what delight, which should it attain its highest point, would become something no longer of this life." Surely he must have been one of the loneliest men of his time, for there were few with whom he could converse either of his theological insights or of his mystical experience. Nevertheless, as mystic he knew the immediacy of God and was comforted by the inward companionship which never cloys and never ends.

Chapter IX

The Philosophical Mysticism of Meister Eckhart

Researchers of mysticism generally agree that there was a great flowering of the mystical consciousness in the fourteenth century. Following what has been commonly called the dark ages, the renaissance of the spirit preceded that of reason and served no doubt as a stimulant to the latter. There is general consensus that the preeminence in this noble company of mystics in the fourteenth century falls naturally upon Meister Eckhart. He managed somehow to combine towering genius with disarming simplicity.

Little is known about the details of his life. When we meet him in his writings and come upon the influence he had on a distinguished succession of mystics, he is already mature and extraordinarily well integrated. This would appear to be the final stage in the personal development of all great mystics. We know very little of the interior pilgrimage by which he climbed to the heights of the characteristic experience of undifferentiated unity with God and his creation. Most of the great mystics seem to be driven to discover a unifying principle out of an overriding need to resolve some interior conflict or dichotomy. If this was the case with Eckhart, we are not aware of what it was. Perhaps he was one of the exceptions that attest the general rule. He may have been one of those still rarer once-born men whose very constitution from birth reflects stability and balance.

TRAINING AND BACKGROUND

Scholars have arrived at 1260 as the most likely year of
Meister Eckhart's birth and have designated the place Hoch-
heim, near Gotha in Thuringia. His father was apparently a
steward in a knight's castle in this densely forested country,
which accounts for some of the metaphors and symbols he later
used in such a telling way. Studying theology at Cologne, he
came early under the influence of the teaching of both Thomas
Aquinas and Albertus Magnus, whose scholastic framework
was already taking hold and foreshadowing the dominant influence it was to exercise in the church until the present time. In
the light of the question regarding the church's fateful choice of
Aquinas in preference to Augustine as its mentor, it is interesting to note that Eckhart quotes Augustine quite as much as
Aquinas. His formal theological training had already been accepted as the approved tradition of the scholastics, but his
preaching reflects that it was in Augustine that he found a
kindred spirit and recognized a soul brother. Some of the mystical theology of Augustine set his imagination aflame and it was
his dramatic and uninhibited restatement of these truths which
had been confirmed in the deeps of his own experience that led
ultimately to his posthumous excommunication.

Following his studies at Cologne, he returned to the monastery at Erfurt and became its prior, bearing also the title of Vicar
of Thuringia. When he was about forty years of age he did
graduate work at the University of Paris, acquiring the master's
degree which was to be the source of the title Meister which was
to supplant his own Christian name, Johannes, in the course of
time. There had already been such a rooting and grounding in
personal faith, through mystical experiences no doubt, which a
native reticence forbade his sharing, that he could not resist a
sharp condemnation of the hairsplitting and sterile theological
disputation he encountered there: "When I preached at Paris I
declared, and I durst now repeat, that not a man at Paris can
conceive with all his learning what God is in the very meanest
creature, not even in a fly."[44] In 1304 he became provincial of

all the Dominican convents in Saxony, and in 1307 he was made vicar-general of the order in Bohemia. These promotions placed upon him strenuous administrative responsibilities as well as the rigors of extensive and constant travel over roads that must have been quite primitive. He seems to have been blessed not only with a vigorous physical constitution whose stamina was up to the task, but with an equable temperament which enabled him to serve effectively as both supervisor and pastor without incurring jealousy or anxiety.

In choosing an appropriate epithet for the mysticism of Eckhart, we refer to it as philosophical. Though Eckhart was not primarily a philosopher, his mysticism has a philosophical quality about it. Partly this judgment is based on his affinity for dealing with elusive and abstract concepts such as the Godhead, albeit often with homely illustration. Partly it relates to a certain philosophic balance he maintained in presenting his convictions, delineating the coincidence of opposites with subtle apprehension. But it has also been pointed out that he stands in some respects as the fountainhead of German idealism. Hegel acknowledged Eckhart, perhaps more generously than was justified, as the inspiration for his own system, while Hegel's followers expressed much admiration for Eckhart's philosophical insights.

ECKHART THE PREACHER

Despite the fact that Meister Eckhart was capable of perceiving and describing subtle distinctions, it was not as philosopher that he is important to the church. His greatest gift was that of transmitting the good news of the mystical message through the medium of preaching. With Paul he apparently believed passionately in the "foolishness of preaching," and like the apostle he was rewarded with the immediate confirmation of warm response. He was driven to impart to others the truths that had been revealed to him in experience and reflection. Possessed of a superb intellect, he was nevertheless able to translate into homely expression the essence of his faith.

Recalling Phillips Brooks's terse definition that preaching is conveying truth through personality, we must realize that there was something in his presence and manner that supported with contagion the impulse to put truth to the test. The burden of the sermon was invariably love, joy, and peace, and the hearers found the words credible because of the manner of person who spoke them. Despite the lofty themes and the subtlety of ideas, there was a childlike simplicity of expression.

The sermons were lively, characterized by buoyancy and gaiety. Rudolf Otto quotes from one of his Latin writings about the life of God flowing into the life of man. The passage might well have been from one of his sermons:

> Life is a boiling up and pouring out of itself, scalding and melting and bubbling within itself, light penetrating light. For life is as it were a gushing up, a thing welling up in itself, pouring a part of itself into another part, as it runs forth and bubbles over beyond itself.[45]

One cannot write or speak in this way unless authentic experience lies behind the words. Like Jesus, he lived under the urgency of striving to communicate the quality of an interior experience of the Kingdom. In the same way he moves from one metaphor to another, from one parable to another, in an effort to attract to the mystical consciousness those whose personal growth enables them to respond. He has unbelievably good news for all who are able to hear it. Since God already dwells within the soul—nay, *is* the soul—one has but to let God be God and live with him the joyous, radiant life. The message is that the Kingdom of God is within you. Only behold it and rejoice to live in it. "Not to be accustomed to inward, spiritual things is never really to know what God is! To have wine in your cellar and never to drink it, or even inspect it, is not to know whether it is good or not."[46] As Raymond Blakney puts it in his introduction to his translation of some of Eckhart's writings: "He breathed his own endless vitality into the juiceless formulas of orthodox theology with such charm and passion that even the common people heard them gladly."[47]

Through all his preaching runs a vein of humor which must further have endeared him to his congregations. It is not humor for the sake of humor, though one feels that he was the kind of person who enjoyed playfulness, but humor for the sake of letting the thrust of truth break through in an unguarded moment. Like Paul, again, he was prepared to be all things to all men but only to the end that he might by all means save some.

> God desires urgently that you, the creature, get out of his way—as if his own blessedness depended on it. Ah, beloved people, why don't you let God be God in you? What are you afraid of? You get completely out of his way and he will get out of yours—you give up to him and he will give up to you. When both [God and you] have forsaken self, what remains [between you] is an indivisible union. It is in this unity that the Father begets his Son in the secret spring of your nature.[48]

He is by turns light and bantering or bold, with intent to shock:

> What is truth? Truth is something so noble that if God could turn aside from it, I could keep to the truth and let God go.[49]

Or again:

> This is a sure and necessary truth, that he who gives up to God his own will, captures God and binds him, so that God can do nothing but what that person wills! Give your will over completely to God and he will give you his in return, so fully and without reserve, that the will of God shall be your own human will.[50]

DOCTRINE OF THE SOUL

The central theme in the teaching of Eckhart was the basic unity between the human soul and God. The sermons might be said to represent many variations upon this single theme.

> There never was another such union [as between the soul and God], for the soul is nearer to God than it is to the body which makes us human. It is more intimate with him than a drop of water put into a vat of wine, for that would still be water and wine; but here, one is changed into the other so that no creature could ever again detect a difference between them.[51]

In the core of the human soul there is a central silence. It is here that God enters into the soul. "He enters the soul through its core and nothing may touch that core except God himself."[52] The Nicene Creed had spoken of the Son as the only begotten of the Father. But the daring doctrine of Eckhart is that this is an estate to which all may aspire. "God begets his Son through the true unity of the divine nature. See! This is the way: He begets his Son in the core of the soul and is made One with it."[53] Shall not a man love himself profoundly when he knows his own soul to be begotten of the Father? "Cherish in yourself the birth of God, and with it all goodness and comfort, all rapture, reality, and truth will be yours. . . . It is the soul that is especially designed for the birth of God and so it occurs exclusively in the soul, where the Father's child is conceived in the core, the inmost recess, where no idea ever glowed or agent of the soul crept in."[54]

He never tires of ringing the variations on this theme. There is never any equivocation, only an intense, passionate concern to get this crucial point across to his hearers:

> The Father ceaselessly begets his Son, and, what is more, he begets me as his Son—the self-same Son! Indeed, I assert that he begets me not only as his Son but as himself and himself as myself, begetting me in his own nature, his own being. At that inmost Source, I spring from the Holy Spirit and there is one life, one being, one action. All God's works are one and therefore he begets me as he does his Son and without distinction.[55]

The soul, God, the Son all become one at the mysterious core of man. "When the Father begets his Son in me, I am that Son and no other. . . . Thus we are all in the Son and *are* the Son."[56] No preacher was ever more explicit in the bold assertion of man's unity with God. "Why did God become man? So that I might be born to be God—yes—identically God."[57] Nor has any ever proclaimed more exultantly the greatest of good news that in the core of the soul "God is perpetually verdant and flowering with all the joy and glory that is in him. Here is joy so hearty, such inconceivably great joy that no one can ever fully tell it, for in this agent the eternal Father is ceaselessly begetting his eternal Son and the agent is parturient with God's offspring and is itself the Son, by the Father's unique power."[58] He never tires of driving home to any who will listen this one astounding truth: "Therefore one should so live that he is identified with God's Son and so that he is that Son. Between the Son and the soul there is no distinction. . . . The soul that lives in the present Now-moment is the soul in which the Father begets his only begotten Son and in that birth the soul is born again. It is still one birth, however often the soul is reborn in God, as the Father begets his only begotten Son."[59]

This noble birth which takes place in the core of the soul he identifies elsewhere as the birth of the aristocrat, "stamped with the likeness of God." "The image of God is unveiled and free in the open soul of the aristocrat." "He is aristocratic because he is One and knows God and creatures as they are One." "So I say that the aristocrat is one who derives his being, his life, and his happiness from God alone."[60] However lowborn a man may be, he may aspire to this aristocracy of the spirit. And ultimately it is the only aristocracy. What unconscious recollection and association is there here? As a boy, Eckhart would have seen at some distance the aristocrat of the castle in which his father was chief servant. Now he had found the castle in the remote fast-nesses of his own being where he could be his own aristocrat to his own delight and that of God! This aristocrat, born of the Spirit, the only begotten Son of the Father, is to be identified finally as the Father himself.

Blasphemy? How could it be interpreted otherwise except by those in whom the mystical consciousness had been sufficiently developed to make confirmation possible? It is no wonder that Rudolf Otto should have described Eckhart as "the Gothic man" in whom the upreach of longing and aspiration reflected in interior grandeur the cathedrals that were being constructed by hand in contemporary society. He called him also "the man with a Faustian urge"[61] in terms of the spirit. Unhappily, the hierarchy of the church that should have hailed Eckhart's coming was shortly to reject him, while others to come who did not understand him at all were to attribute to him something utterly foreign to his spirit. Alfred Rosenberg in Nazi Germany proclaimed: "In him the Nordic soul for the first time came to a consciousness of itself. From his great soul our German faith can and will be born."[62] Nothing could have been farther removed from the mind and heart of Eckhart than the notion of a master race. He allowed only one aristocracy, and this the natural heritage of any who will claim it.

Like the mystics generally, Eckhart spoke not only to the condition of his contemporaries but to people of goodwill in every age. He speaks with peculiar clarity to our post-Darwinian space age by pointing to that within the soul which lies beyond both time and space. The point omega, if there be one, of the entire evolutionary process is already present in the soul.

> To get at the core of God at his greatest, one must first get into the core of himself at his least, for no one can know God who has not first known himself. Go to the depths of the soul, the secret place of the Most High, to the roots, to the heights; for all that God can do is focused there.[63]

If there is a disconcerting displacement in our faith when we discover that no God is to be found "out there" in space, we need not be alarmed, since God is to be known and embraced with blessed assurance "in here." A man is to "find his unity and blessing in that little spark in the soul, which neither space nor time touches."[64] Here is to be found a light that

> wants to penetrate the simple core, the still desert, into which no distinction ever crept—neither the Father, the Son, nor the Holy Spirit. It wants to get into the secret, to which no man is privy, where it is satisfied by a Light whose unity is greater than its own. This core is a simple stillness, which is unmoved itself but by whose immobility all things are moved and all receive life, that is to say, all people who live by reason and have their center within themselves.[65]

There follows swiftly, as if in the same breath, the prayer: "That we, too, may live so intelligently, may God help us. Amen."

By insisting that we see behind and beyond the trinity of the Father, Son, and Holy Spirit the unfathomable and ineffable unity of the Godhead, Eckhart reconstructed a bridge, always in need of repair, between philosophy and theology. At the same time he opened the way to genuine communication with other living religions, so necessary to explore in our time. It could be said that Augustine and Eckhart, in moving from the Christ-mysticism of Paul toward a form more properly described as God-mysticism, performed a service to religion. In so doing, they helped to remove or at least to underplay what must inevitably constitute a stumbling block to those of other religions, and perhaps to many Christians as well, who long to universalize their faith and to free the Jesus of history from the accumulated weight of theological overlay.

ECKHART'S TEACHING ON SIN AND EVIL

Although Eckhart fearlessly and exultantly strikes always the positive note concerning the inexhaustible riches that lie so close at hand for the believer, he does not deny the appalling reality of sin and evil. If God dwells alone in the core of the soul, it is still quite possible for the "Devil" to seize and take possession, working all manner of evil in and through the person. The light still shines in the darkness, but the darkness of itself cannot comprehend it. Eckhart no less than any other mystic knows that the way to proficiency and ultimate illumination is through rigorous purging, yet he never approves of self-flagellation. What is required is a turning away from sin.

> There is no way of making a person true unless he gives up his own will. In fact, apart from complete surrender of the will, there is no traffic with God.[66]

Nevertheless, once a person in affection and longing turns to God, it matters not how great were the person's past sins. No one's forgiveness is so complete as God's.

> Even if your sins were as great in number as all mankind's put together, still he would not count them against you and he would still have as much confidence in you as he ever had in any creature. If only he finds you ready, he will pay no attention to what you were before. God is God of the present; as he finds a man, so he takes him and accepts him, not for what he has been but for what he is now.[67]

What is required is to turn steadily toward God in love:

> Love knows nothing of sin—not that man has not sinned—but sins
> are blotted out at once by love and they vanish as if they had not
> been. This is because whatever God does he does completely, like
> the cup running over. Whom he forgives, he forgives utterly and at
> once, much preferring great forgiveness to little; for complete confi-
> dence is like that.[68]

It is also a matter of getting one's self out of the way, so that
place may be made for God.

> To the extent that you eliminate self from your activities, God
> comes into them—but not more and no less. Begin with that, and
> let it cost you your uttermost. In this way, and no other, is true
> peace to be found.[69]

Another way of putting it is the cultivation of disinterest:

> When I survey the virtues, I find none as flawless, as conducive to
> God as disinterest. . . . You may take this for the truth, that when
> a free mind is really disinterested, God is compelled to come into
> it. . . . Know, then, that a mind unmoved by any contingent affection
> or sorrow, or honor, or slander, or vice, is really disinterested—like
> a broad mountain that is not shaken by a gentle wind. Unmovable
> disinterest brings a man into his closest resemblance to God. It gives
> God his status as God. . . . Keep this in mind: to be full of things
> is to be empty of God, while to be empty of things is to be full of
> God.[70]

THE INFLUENCE OF ECKHART

It is characteristic of the mystic that the doctrines which
congeal from the molten lava of experience have a boldness that
strikes others as excessive, if not dangerous. When we considered the aberrations and vagaries of mysticism in an earlier
chapter we noted that it is not surprising that the authorities
should view with alarm the teachings of the mystics. When
anyone in an ecstatic moment proclaims "My me is God," it is
not only popes and bishops that become anxious but modern
psychologists as well. It all depends in what spirit the words are
spoken—the sermon that is preached by the life of the person

above and beyond and behind the words. Hubris instead of humility may accompany them, illusion instead of inspiration. With Eckhart there seems to have been no question of authenticity on either count. But it is true that it takes a mystic to recognize and to respond to one. To those in whom the mystical faculty has not been developed, mysticism may well seem dangerous heresy.

One of the ironies about the charges of heresy that were brought against Eckhart, however understandable on the surface, was that the movement to excommunicate him was initiated by men in the rival order of the Franciscans. What an embarrassment this would have been to Francis of Assisi, who would have recognized in Eckhart on sight a brother in Christ! One remembers the wistful query of General Booth of the Salvation Army, as a result of his own experience, "Why is it that God cannot keep a movement pure for more than one generation?"

There is a touching similarity between Eckhart and Teilhard. Both came under fire during their lifetime. Both cherished a profound sense of loyalty to their respective orders and did not think of themselves as heretical. For twenty years Teilhard suffered virtual banishment from the intellectual circles of his church on which since his death he is having increasing influence. Eckhart was actually found guilty of heresy after his death and was posthumously excommunicated, if such an interdict is possible. The citation brought against him charged that he "incited ignorant and undisciplined people to wild and dangerous excesses." A bill of particulars was drawn up by those who were chosen to pursue the inquisition. One can imagine the poignancy of Eckhart's interior sorrow as he set about responding with meticulous care. His defense is as free of petulance and bitterness as were the letters and utterances of Teilhard during his long rejection.

The defense was summed up in one magnificent response: "I may err but I may not be a heretic—for the first has to do with the mind and the second with the will!"[71] He admitted that he had said and written the specific words and that he might indeed be in error, but, far from recanting, he said with measured words and characteristic serenity: "I think . . . that they are all true, although many of them are rare, difficult and subtle."[2] Then he promptly made appeal to Rome, but it was denied. Death came mercifully before he was officially found guilty of heresy. The bull of Pope John XXII of March 27, 1329, speaks of him as dead. It condemns him on twenty-six points, seventeen of which are said to be heretical, the others dubious and indiscreet, and refers to him as having been deceived "by the father of lies who often appears as an angel of light" into "sowing thorns and thistles amongst the faithful and even the simple folk." Fortunately, he who was concerned only to set the common people free was spared that final humiliation.

Despite the controversy that clouded the last days of his life, Eckhart's preaching and teaching had won spontaneous response from the movement known as the Friends of God. He had great influence upon Tauler and Suso in particular and upon others who were to follow. It is true that the official condemnation precluded the canonization that he merited and kept his teaching for centuries from enjoying the influence it would certainly have had upon many receptive spirits.

Eckhart is of special importance to us today. His form of philosophical mysticism is cast in metaphors that can speak to mystics of the Eastern religions as well as those of the West. He has a perspective curiously compatible with the current one of biological space-time or duration which Teilhard holds we must embrace if we are to be truly modern men. I do not find Raymond Blakney's claim extravagant: "He lived . . . on the same highlands of the spirit that were disclosed in the Upanishads and Sufi classics. To go where Eckhart went is to come close to Lao Tzu and Buddha, and certainly to Jesus Christ."

Certainly he set the Christian faith to a quality of music it has rarely enjoyed. Because he occupies an important place in the authentic apostolic succession, he has quickened poetic and devotional expression from his day to ours. Johann Scheffler, who wrote under the pen name of Angelus Silesius, in the middle of the seventeenth century undertook to reproduce in poetic form some of the music he heard in Eckhart. In a poem entitled

"In Thine Own Heart," Scheffler reflects one of Eckhart's great mystical insights:

> Though Christ a thousand times
>   In Bethlehem be born,
> If He's not born in thee
>   Thy soul is still forlorn.
> The cross on Golgotha
>   Will never save thy soul,
> The cross in thine own heart
>   Alone can make thee whole.

Chapter X
The Material Mysticism of Teilhard de Chardin

The mystic is under greater constraint than others. He must not merely perceive connections between apparently disparate things and ideas, but make one of two or more worlds which he experiences as in deadly conflict within him. All men have interior divisions and are prone to autonomous complexes which may be out of touch with or in direct opposition to the real identity. For the mystic, however, the struggle for identity and integrity assumes epic, even cosmic, proportions because it presents itself existentially as an intensely personal life-and-death struggle. He becomes a mystic precisely because he experiences a breakthrough in terms of a unifying principle, a coincidence of opposites, an overarching integration in which conflicting worlds become one world. He impresses his fellows as both strangely at home in the world and mysteriously at peace within himself. It is as if the mystic's integrity (and this may be the dominant impression the mystic makes upon others) is achieved because he has suffered, at least in imagination, a potential dichotomy that threatens to tear him to pieces.

THE INTERIOR CONFLICT REQUIRING RESOLUTION

What was this confrontation for Teilhard? It was the potential conflict between Teilhard the priest and man of faith, and Teilhard the scientist. It was the conflict between reality as he was learning to perceive it through his study of paleontology and reality as the church had traditionally understood and interpreted it. He had embraced the teaching of the church and its faith in the God of Jesus the Christ in such a way that he could not contemplate abandoning this faith without in some sense ceasing to exist. At the same time, he had made an early interior commitment to the validity of scientific observation and the inductive method of arriving at knowledge. The traditional dualism of matter and spirit constituted for him an intolerable conflict. Nor could he accept any kind of compromise that would keep the two worlds in airtight compartments. He experienced the mystic's characteristic compulsion to reach for the conjunction of opposites. This motivation drove him to daring scientific and theological speculation.

His experience in the First World War intensified the interior quest because of his direct encounter with violence, hatred, and suffering. What is the meaning of evil in a world created by a good God of whom Jesus is the central revelation? But for Teilhard the greater conflict was the philosophical one of meaninglessness versus purposefulness in the process of evolution itself. The more he explored the implications of an evolving universe, the more an alternative confronted him with the specter of an angst of monumental proportions. In pointing to modern man's dilemma he is indirectly confessing the crisis he had once experienced so acutely:

> The child is terrified when it opens its eyes for the first time. Similarly, for our mind to adjust itself to lines and horizons enlarged beyond measure, it must renounce the comfort of familiar narrowness. It must create a new equilibrium for everything that had formerly been so neatly arranged in its small inner world. It is dazzled when it emerges from its dark prison, awed to find itself suddenly at the top of a tower, and it suffers from giddiness and disorientation. The whole psychology of modern disquiet is linked with the sudden confrontation with space-time. . . . Conscious or not, suppressed anguish—a fundamental anguish of being—despite our smiles, strikes in the depths of all our hearts and is the undertone of all our conversations. . . . In the first and most widespread degree, the "malady of space-time" manifests itself as a rule by a feeling of futility, of being crushed by the enormities of the cosmos.[73]

Teilhard finds the "complement and necessary corrective" to this malady "the perception of an evolution animating those

dimensions. . . . Indeed time and space become humanised as
soon as a definite movement appears which gives them a physi-
ognomy."[74] For this "sickness of the dead end—the anguish of
feeling shut in" and of "not being sure, and not seeing how it
[the world] ever could be sure, that there is an outcome—*a
suitable outcome*—to that evolution" there is a remedy: "We
have only to think and to walk in the direction in which the lines
passed by evolution take on their maximum coherence."[75]

The conflict was resolved not merely by the achievement of
an intellectual synthesis. There was involved also a profound act
of trust. Teilhard committed himself not only into the keeping
of an eternal God. What other saint had not done as much? His
distinctive achievement was committing himself in trust to the
world as well, the very world that many churchmen had characteristically distrusted. Here is the way he put it:

> If, as a result of some interior revolution, I were successfully to lose
> my faith in Christ, my faith in a personal God, my faith in the Spirit,
> I think that I would still continue to believe in the World. The
> World (the value, the infallibility, the goodness of the World): that,
> in the final analysis, is the first and the last thing in which I believe.
> It is by this faith that I believe. It is by this faith that I live, and it
> is to this faith, I feel, that at the moment of death, mastering all
> doubts, I shall surrender myself. I surrender myself to this un-
> defined faith in a single and Infallible World, wherever it may lead
> me.[76]

Such a rhapsodic confidence in the world itself can only be
understood in the context of the basic mystical experience which
seems to have taken place not once but repeatedly throughout
his life.

> Throughout my life, through my life, the world has little by little
> caught fire in my sight until, aflame all around me, it has become
> almost completely luminous from within. . . . Such has been my
> experience in contact with the earth—the diaphany of the divine at
> the heart of the universe on fire . . . Christ; His heart; a fire: capable
> of penetrating everywhere and, gradually, spreading everywhere.[77]

It is because of this central and continuing mystical experience that we have chosen to entitle this chapter "The Material

Mysticism of Teilhard de Chardin." Certainly his mysticism is spiritual. It is poetic. It is aesthetic. But what more than anything else distinguishes it from others in the succession is that it springs from the way in which he perceives matter as the channel through which spirit flows and is released. It is in matter that he experiences the diaphany of the divine. Schweitzer realized the mystic impulse from a sense of reverence for life. Wordsworth found a presence in all of nature, in "the light of setting suns, and the round ocean and the living air, and the blue sky, and in the mind of man." But from a boy Teilhard had experienced the numinous in "bits of iron, a ploughshare, the top of a metal pillar, a piece of shell from the range."[78] No one has succeeded so well in eliminating any sense of conflict between matter and spirit. He had succeeded in "Christifying" matter, divinizing it in his own interior attitude. The two great compositions that were to come later, *La Messe sur le Monde* in 1923 and *Le Milieu Divin* in 1927, were but extensions in idea and imagination of the characteristic relationship to the world that his mystical experience had made possible.

THE WITHIN OF THINGS

This reverence for matter as distinct from mere reverence for life sprang from and reinforced the Teilhardian vision of a cosmogenesis from which has already arisen biogenesis, and more recently noogenesis. Each successive development has come in the fullness of time, but only because each was, as it were, asleep in matter from the beginning. Evolution can be measured in its progress by ascending levels of consciousness. But this very *within* of matter is to be understood in terms of a primitive or unawakened consciousness awaiting conditions in the evolving environment favorable for its denouement and further development. In one place he describes the process in this way: "The universe in gravitation fell forward upon Spirit, as upon its stable form."[79] This process came to fruition in man. But the potential was always present in matter. So the incarnation can be seen as far deeper and infinitely earlier than the church ever dreamed before. The incarnation was concurrent with the creation of matter itself. In *Le Coeur de la Matière* he confesses that "starting from an inherited spark of light, the world during all my life and by means of all my life has gradually become entirely luminous from within."[80]

As for all mystics, the more important dimension was the immanence of God. The divine is immanent not only in man but in matter itself. The transcendence of God becomes not so much a matter of spatial separation (the way it had usually been conceived) as one within time, more accurately space-time. Through the Christogenesis that has been taking place in matter all along, but has now become visible in man, the whole universe is on its way to point omega when Jesus as Christ shall come into his own and reign supreme forever and ever. Thus is God in a sense as near as matter and as distant as the fulfillment of the whole process of evolution.

But man is not merely an onlooker. One paradox is that, though the whole process has been so designed and so guarded and nurtured from the beginning that Jesus could emerge from the heart of matter, in some sense Jesus as the Christ and God are both dependent upon man's continued moral effort in this present. One feels in Teilhard that the final realization of point omega, "the Christification of the universe," is somehow assured, and yet that it will be attained only through the obedience and sustained commitment of the faithful, even somehow through the proper performance of and participation in the Eucharist. We work within time for the fulfillment of that which comes in the fullness of time. And yet, as man was once contained within a tree shrew and in still more primitive forms of life, and even before that in matter, so the seed of the ultimate Christification of the universe rests safely within the womb of matter. This leap of faith, his final conclusion, is initiated and supported by his own mystical consciousness. This does not mean, however, that he was not aware of the risks he was running, as is attested by the words:

> Bit by bit, under the synthetic influence of experience, detachment and attachment, renunciation and development began to join up automatically in a sort of meeting point of which in 1927 I gave the

explanation in the first chapter of the *Milieu Divin*. . . . The explanation is not always practicable. Even today I have not finished exploring the dangers to which man is exposed when by inner constraint he sees himself compelled to leave the beaten track of traditional discipline, now for him sub-human, and look for a road to heaven wherein the whole energy of Matter and Flesh can pass into the birth of Spirit.[81]

THE TEILHARDIAN VISION

The Teilhardian vision is a staggering one. As one stretches mind and spirit to encompass it, one inevitably experiences the kind of dizziness and malaise that Teilhard himself seems to be alluding to in such a passage. One recognizes the possibility of slipping into the grip of a great illusion, however irresistible. Freud's charge against the Christian religion, that of projecting the father image, seems scarcely adequate to such a frame of reference. One wonders how he would have diagnosed Teilhard's condition! When, however, one recalls the characteristic compulsion of the religious instinct to interrelate everything one knows and experiences in one world view, the main lines of the Teilhardian vision seem inevitable. Indeed, they seem inescapable, given an experienced, Christ-centered mysticism and the extension of the evolutionary concept to embrace all existence in the cosmos from the first atom up to mankind.

Among the words Teilhard coined, none is more appealing than "hominization." Man is on the way to becoming man, but he has not yet arrived. Man's continuing evolution is a process of hominization. What if there should be failure? What if suicide or extinction befall man as a result of atomic warfare, or unchecked pollution, or overpopulation, or some combination of the three? What if the species should become extinct, as others have, through our own version of overspecialization in which technological advance outstrips the slower pace of the development of conscience and human-heartedness? Will some other species, here or elsewhere, pick up and preserve the Ariadne thread? Teilhard did not think so. He inclined to feel that as there was only one moment in time, as it were, when conditions were just right for the transformation of certain albumen amalgamations into the first cell, so there will not be another chance for the kind of breakthrough which mind experienced in the development of man. Man is the pinnacle of the evolutionary process, not only on this planet but in the universe as well. As such he is irreplaceable. When one considers how distinct were the various species which developed on this planet in those places where no land bridges existed, it is difficult to conceive how there could have been a concurrent development of evolution on any other planet that would allow for the presence of any other thinking animal, a contemporary of man, even should any form of life exist elsewhere, as would seem highly likely.

One may fairly raise the question whether any form of eschatology or faith concerning the last things is compatible with the evolutionary process. Is not any kind of eschatological concept an anachronistic imposition upon evolution, occasioned by the mind-set that has long imagined such an end? Ever since the seers of the Old Testament we have looked for a Kingdom of God on earth. The mind boggles at the prospect of endless evolution into states of being we cannot imagine. Our very mental orientation and the slender tolerances of sanity seem almost to demand a denouement, a point omega. But is there anything in the nature of the process itself, apart from our natural juxtaposition of a final attainment, that points to such an end of itself? I am inclined to think not. This is not to say that we cannot and indeed must not envision what we can of the new man and the new society, as far ahead as imagination and inspiration can carry us. The vision will necessarily serve us as a practical point omega toward which to bend our moral and spiritual efforts. But must we not contemplate the possibility, even the likelihood, of unimagined worlds beyond that dimly imagined world?

The Christification of the universe as the point omega! I am sure I only partially grasp the vision that was Teilhard's when the seer "got it all together" and presented it to us in his essays and papers. But the quality of life he identified as the love of Christ I too am prepared to acknowledge as the highest value that man has yet experienced, worthy alone of adoration. I too believe that such love has within it a power of attraction and of transformation that, within its own sphere, is as great as atomic energy and is only beginning to be made manifest. That such a spiritual reality should have emerged from the very heart of matter is enough of an incarnation to hold me in thrall the rest of my days.

Considering the staggering acceleration of the pace of change within the past few decades in so many fields of human endeavor, the distance we can look ahead with any confidence seems rather to shorten than to expand. I cannot really comprehend what a Christification of the universe might mean. I can grasp a little of what some steps toward the Christification of the Family of Man on this planet would involve. War as a projection and implementation of national, ideological, or ethnic policies must be banished once and for all from the face of the earth. All death-dealing weapons must be forgone by all for the sake of the species. Population must be kept within agreed-upon limits, if not reduced, so that the earth may support other living species as well as man. The pollution of air and water and earth must cease. These are the negative requirements, apart from which all other positive movements might in the end prove abortive.

Concurrently with progress on these fronts, however, there must be a major breakthrough in human trust. There must be a worldwide propagation of the Teilhardian evolutionary axiom for our times. "The age of nations is past. The task before us, if we would not perish, is to build the earth." We must reclaim the earth as a beautiful and gracious home for man and other creatures. There must be a great advance in the human care of human beings, giving the existing energies of compassion free range to quicken and to nurture human-heartedness everywhere. Scientific and psychological research must expand through great corporate efforts on an international and intercultural basis. Models of what cooperative and coordinated research can accomplish are already at hand in both medicine and space probing. We have yet to apply the same disciplined effort of our best minds, supported by adequate financial resources, in other areas of human need and interest.

Men violently disagree as to desirable and viable social structures both as means to envisioned social ends and as social ends in themselves. The conflict between the Communism of the East and what has been euphemistically called the Free World by the West is not merely one of system—economic, social, or political —but of value placed upon styles of life. Fabulous human as well as economic resources have been expended upon the cold war for the last thirty years when they should have been directed toward resolving problems that confront the entire species. Moreover, the cold war, having developed the weapons of deterrence, still threatens, if only by accident, to become a hot war engulfing the world.

CHRISTIFICATION OR HOMINIZATION

Threatened by the prospect of our own extinction as a species, through developments and movements that have gotten out of control, we must now reflect upon what resources we may have to stem the existing tides of self-destruction. These resources, I believe, lie at the heart of the world's great living religions, including the most recent in the great company, one which Julian Huxley has named evolutionary humanism. The highest common denominator in all these religions, constituting the central means of communication between them, is the mystical consciousness. This is the capacity, not only to identify and to empathize with all men everywhere, but to experience the immanence of God in man and in the rest of creation. Just as he believed the age of nations was past, Teilhard also believed that the age of religions is past and that we are about to embark upon the age of religion.

Though the best in other religions will be converging upon the axis of the Christian phylum, Teilhard saw Christianity as having inherited and therefore bearing the burden of man's continuing evolution in mind and spirit. It is at this point that I would quarrel somewhat with Teilhard. In the first place, I think he ought to have distinguished more clearly than he did between the Jesus of history and the Christ of theology. For all his genius in placing everything within the context of space-time, he did not see that men have successively foisted upon the historic figure of Jesus the growing weight of the archetypal image of the perfect man. Jesus might well have rejected this thrust, if some of his intuitive responses in Scripture to the adulation of his followers are any indication. One might have thought that Teilhard, of all persons, would have insisted upon keeping separate the man Jesus and what was incarnate in him in the shape of the promise of the new man.

As man evolves, there is bound to be prefigured from time to time, as a kind of bodhisattva (to borrow the symbol of another religion), the characteristics of the new man. I am surprised that Teilhard did not seize the metaphor that Jesus himself used, "son of man," and the one Paul conjured up, "firstborn among many brethren," and make more of their coincidental relevance to the evolutionary perspective. Perhaps he might have identified the theological Christ figure with the fully hominized man that is to be and suggested that this Christ figure indwelt Jesus of Nazareth to a larger degree than any other historic personage.

Instead, he appears to have accepted fully the identification of the Jesus of history and the Christ of theology as if they were one and the same entity. No doubt this was an unconscious projection onto the cosmic plane of what remained to the end a very simple and single-minded piety, despite the sophistication of the scientific element in his vision. But this limitation, I am afraid, will block rather than attract many in other living religions who might otherwise have been won to the sweep and scope of his evolutionary concept. I personally wish he had spoken only of *divinization* and *hominization* of the universe instead of its *Christification,* a term that is bound to create a psychological barrier to those of other faiths. Had he spoken of the Holy Spirit as constituting the diaphany of the divine in Jesus of Nazareth who was the firstborn of many brethren in whom the family likeness will manifest itself—this would have been acceptable to philosopher-theologians like Sri Aurobindo of other living faiths who had already assimilated in their world view the perspective of space-time. Jesus the sport, the new man, the Son of Man, man's successor, the first fully hominized man!

The spirit that was in Jesus, in any evolutionary scheme, is bound to have its recurring incarnation in others who are to follow. Until such another emerges we are bound to look to Jesus of Nazareth as the prototype of the man who is to be. More than any other man who has ever lived he mirrors to us the unlived Christ life we dimly know to be stirring within the depths of our own being. Nevertheless, to foster the kind of communication and common cause so needed among the religions of the world today it would be well for us to make this distinction very clear. Others too have the archetypal image of the good man, the nonviolent man, the man for others, at once gentle and strong, compassionate and passionate, contemplative and activist. Let us call him the new man who has emerged in Jesus, but also in other men, and who will continue to emerge, the brethren of whom we have known some of the firstborn, the brethren who are now spread over the face of the earth.

It is strange that one so venturesome in his scientific thought remained so cautious in some areas of his theological thinking. No doubt this was largely because of his profound loyalty to the Jesuit order of which he was a member. It would seem that the assimilation of the concept of duration by all disciplines, including the history of religions, the necessity of which he never tired of preaching, would have demanded of him a more explicit rejection of the traditional doctrines of the Virgin Birth, the Incarnation, the Redemption, and the Resurrection, not merely of the Fall. The logical application and extension of his perspective into these areas of doctrinal interpretation would have necessitated public rejection of traditional views, one might have expected. One suspects that he did not force the issues lest he appear to be rejecting more than he intended. Meanwhile, perhaps he was content to make peace with himself on the ground that he was retaining the doctrines as metaphors of spiritual reality rather than as statements to be understood literally. Moreover, like Eckhart, he was unable to contemplate final excommunication from what he called his "divine milieu."

TEILHARD THE APOLOGIST

Despite his reticence in these areas, Teilhard remains the greatest apologist for the Christian faith in our post-Darwinian period. He succeeded to a remarkable degree in following the counsel of Alexander von Humboldt, contemporary and friend of Goethe:

> The thoughtful scientist's most important achievement is this: to recognize unity in diversity, to comprehend all that the discoveries of recent times tell us about the individual, to sift and scrutinize details without succumbing beneath their weight, and, *mindful of man's high destiny, to perceive the spirit of Nature,* which lies hidden beneath a covering of external phenomena. In this way, our endeavors will reach beyond the narrow confines of the external world and we shall succeed in mastering the raw material of empirical observation, as it were, by ideas.[82]

The particular form of prophecy that is especially needed in our time is a new apology for the faith that will take into its ken the frontiers of scientific thought, relate them to one another on an interdisciplinary basis, and remythologize the faith so as to present a plausible theory of the way in which all the elements hang together. Since it was primarily the discovery of the process of evolution and the subsequent understanding of that process as coextensive with time and space (revealing as yet no knowledge of either beginning or end) that has shaken the foundations of religious faith, the most crucial work has been the reestablishment of foundations that will support the thought and faith of twentieth-century man. No one has contributed more to this end than Teilhard. He did indeed practice what he preached. He saw to it that the lines of his own theology and Christology at least began "to follow that curve." As Julian Huxley put it in his introduction to *The Phenomenon of Man,* Teilhard "effected a threefold synthesis—of the material and physical world with the world of mind and spirit; of the past with the future; and of variety with unity, the many with the one."[83]

Teilhard himself, considering his objective and sense of mission, summed up for us his appraisal of the core of his message for modern man in these words:

> Religion and science are the two conjugated faces or phases of one and the same act of complete knowledge—the only one which can embrace the past and future of evolution so as to contemplate, measure and fulfil them.
>
> In the mutual reinforcement of these two still opposed powers, in the conjunction of reason and mysticism, the human spirit is destined, by the very nature of its development, to find the uttermost degree of its penetration with the maximum of its vital force.[84]

Note that the religion which can and must unite with science is a form of mysticism. Dean Inge had prophesied some years ago that what Christianity required for its revitalization was a new form of Platonism, appropriate to the times. How he would have rejoiced in the achievement of Teilhard! So hardy is the perennial philosophy of mysticism that it can burst forth even in that soil where Aristotle has long held sway! Speaking of the incomprehensible power of Christian love, Teilhard asks:

> Is it not a positive fact that thousands of mystics, for twenty centuries, have drawn from its flame a passionate fervour that outstrips by far in brightness and purity the urge and devotion of any human love? Is it not also a fact that, having once experienced it, further thousands of men and women are daily renouncing every other ambition and every other joy save that of abandoning themselves to it and labouring within it more and more completely?[85]

If the church were really profoundly involved in being about "the Father's business" today, its central concern would be the making of mystics, great contemplatives, both within and detached from the mainstream of urban life. The phenomenon of Teilhard himself has convinced some of us that the church must produce more and more men and women capable of praying as he counseled:

> To be able to say literally to God that one loves him, not only with all one's body, all one's heart and all one's soul, but with every fibre of the unifying universe—that is a prayer that can only be made in space-time.[86]

And what he wrote to his devoted friend, Léontine Zanta, we may well take to heart as if directed to us personally:

Make good the deficiencies you feel by redoubling your inner life, your "mystical vision."[87]

Conclusion

This book has been written in the passionate conviction that the Christian church is itself in need of salvation in our day, and that the saving word and life have been preserved in the authentic apostolic succession of mystics from Jesus to Teilhard de Chardin and C. G. Jung. The church has always been wary of its mystics. By turns it has exalted as ultimate authority hierarchy, ritual, and literal interpretation of Scripture. The only authority to which the church can now turn with any confidence and credibility before the world is the authority of that direct interior religious experience which is the peculiar testimony of Christian mysticism. The mystics are the only apologists for the faith to whom modern men and women will listen with respect, however grudgingly.

The perspective of biological space-time finds neo-orthodoxy and the so-called salvation history of Biblical theology irrelevant. The perspective of depth psychology rules out literal understanding of the classic kerygma and finds it in our time more productive of neurosis than health of body, mind, and spirit. At the same time, many first-class minds among scientists and psychologists are prepared to listen attentively to the witness of the mystics.

I will yield to none in my equally passionate concern for social reform. I was an ardent participant in the revolutionary movement for civil rights as long as it remained committed to nonviolence and integration under the inspired leadership of Martin Luther King, Jr. I have long been a Christian pacifist by conviction. I aspire to remain loyal to the Gandhian principles applied to all forms of direct social action. At the same time, I believe the greatest single need of the church is currently to acknowledge the authentic continuity of Christian mysticism and to accord it the place of preeminence it has always deserved and never been granted. Since sound mysticism is itself the primary source of the deepest compassion, wise and sacrificial involvement in movements for revolutionary social reform will inevitably follow for those who identify with it.

Hence I have undertaken to set forth what I understand to be the nature of salutary mystical experience, within the Christian tradition, and its relevance to our time. Limitations of space precluded consideration of more than five of the mystics in the apostolic succession whose numbers are recorded only in heaven. Nevertheless, it is hoped that the swift survey of the distinctive perspective and teaching of these few will serve to suggest the infinite range and variety among them. At the same time, they share a peculiar similarity that causes one to reflect that if "the saints do not disagree," still less do the mystics in all important matters of faith.

The experience they labor to describe in many metaphors is basically one and the same. The mystical faculty, it is maintained, constitutes the growing edge of continuing evolution in man. All who recognize themselves as having experienced the mystical consciousness in any degree or in any area of human experience will find here, it is hoped, something with which they can genuinely identify on a deep level of aspiration and hope. What the church desperately needs is an apologetic which will be able to retain the respect of its present members and to draw others into its currently diminishing fold. I am persuaded that for an effective apologetic for our time we must turn to the living waters in the reservoir of Christian mysticism.

Notes

1. Raymond B. Blakney, *Meister Eckhart, A Modern Translation* (Harper & Brothers, 1941; first Harper Torchbook edition, 1957), p. xxi.
2. Pierre Teilhard de Chardin, *The Phenomenon of Man* (Harper & Brothers, 1959), pp. 217f.
3. J. Bronowski (ed.), *William Blake* (Penguin Books, 1961), p. 11.
4. Emily Herman, *The Meaning and Value of Mysticism* (1922), p. 3.
5. W. R. Inge, *Christian Mysticism* (1899), p. 5.
6. Evelyn Underhill, *Mysticism* (1911), pp. xiv–xv.
7. Walter T. Stace, *The Teachings of the Mystics* (New American Library, Inc., 1960), p. 20.
8. Inge, *Christian Mysticism*, p. 21.
9. Herman, *The Meaning and Value of Mysticism*, pp. 26f.
10. Plotinus, *Ennead* vi.7.34.
11. Stace, *The Teachings of the Mystics*, pp. 26f.
12. Albert Schweitzer, *Out of My Life and Thought* (Holt, Rinehart & Winston, Inc., 1972), pp. 185f.
13. Martin Buber, *Between Man and Man* (The Macmillan Company, 1965), p. 3.
14. Pierre Teilhard de Chardin, *The Divine Milieu* (Harper & Brothers, 1960), p. 14, Editor's Note.
15. Charles W. Williams, *The Descent of the Dove* (Wm. B. Eerdmans Publishing Company, 1965), p. 108.
16. Albert Schweitzer, *The Psychiatric Study of Jesus* (The Beacon Press, 1950).
17. James Naylor, *Works, To the Life of God in All*, pp. xxxix–xlix.
18. *Ibid.*, p. 696.
19. Teilhard de Chardin, *The Phenomenon of Man*, p. 218.
20. Albert Schweitzer, *The Quest of the Historical Jesus* (A. & C. Black, Ltd., London, 1936), p. 401.

21. *Ibid.*, pp. 2f.
22. *Ibid.*
23. *Ibid.*
24. *Ibid.*, p. 3.
25. Henry Cadbury, *The Eclipse of the Historical Jesus* (Pendle Hill Pamphlet #133), p. 18.
26. *Ibid.*, pp. 26f.
27. *Ibid.*, p. 27.
28. Quoted in Cadbury, *The Eclipse of the Historical Jesus,* p. 28.
29. Albert Schweitzer, *The Mysticism of Paul the Apostle* (The Macmillan Company, 1955), pp. 376f.
30. *Ibid.*, p. 1.
31. *Ibid.*, p. 3.
32. *Ibid.*, p. 378.
33. *Ibid.*
34. *Ibid.*
35. *Ibid.*, p. 379.
36. *Ibid.*, pp. 395f.
37. Ignatius, *Ad Ephesians* 11.1.
38. Schweitzer, *The Mysticism of Paul the Apostle,* p. 373.
39. Giovanni Papini, *Saint Augustine* (Harcourt, Brace and Company, 1930), pp. 18f.
40. *Ibid.*, p. 22.
41. Augustine, *The Confessions,* Book II, Ch. 2, trans. in Papini, *Saint Augustine,* pp. 45f.
42. Papini, *Saint Augustine,* p. 140.
43. Augustine, *Confessions,* Book IX, Ch. 10, trans. in Papini, *Saint Augustine.*
44. Franz Pfeiffer, *Meister Eckhart,* tr. by C. de B. Evans (London: John M. Watkins, 1924), Vol. I, p. 133.
45. Rudolf Otto, *Mysticism East and West* (The Macmillan Company, 1970), p. 171, fn. 4.
46. Blakney, *Meister Eckhart,* p. 216.
47. *Ibid.*, p. xxviii.
48. *Ibid.*, p. 127.
49. *Ibid.*, p. 240.
50. *Ibid.*, p. 175.
51. *Ibid.*, p. 29.
52. *Ibid.*, p. 97.
53. *Ibid.*, p. 98.
54. *Ibid.*, pp. 103f.

55. *Ibid.,* p. 181.
56. *Ibid.,* p. 186. (Emphasis added.)
57. *Ibid.,* p. 194.
58. *Ibid.,* p. 209.
59. *Ibid.,* pp. 213f.
60. *Ibid.,* pp. 76, 77, 78, 79, 80.
61. Otto, *Mysticism East and West,* p. 181.
62. Alfred Rosenberg, *Der Mythus des 20. Jahrhunderts* (Munich, 1930).
63. Blakney, *Meister Eckhart,* p. 346.
64. *Ibid.,* p. 246.
65. *Ibid.,* p. 247.
66. *Ibid.,* p. 16.
67. *Ibid.,* p. 18.
68. *Ibid.,* p. 21.
69. *Ibid.,* p. 6.
70. *Ibid.,* pp. 84f.
71. Blakney, *Meister Eckhart,* p. xxiii.
72. *Ibid.,* p. 259.
73. Teilhard de Chardin, *The Phenomenon of Man,* pp. 225f.
74. *Ibid.,* p. 227.
75. *Ibid.,* pp. 227, 233.
76. Pierre Teilhard de Chardin, Article in *L'Osservatore Romano,* July 1, 1962, p. 132.
77. Teilhard de Chardin, *The Divine Milieu,* p. 14, Editor's Note.
78. P. Leroy, *Teilhard de Chardin, tel que je l'ai connu,* p. 11; *Letters,* p. 20.
79. Pierre Teilhard de Chardin, *Le Coeur de la Matière* (Paris: Editions du Seuil), Autobiographical Papers, unpublished essay.
80. *Ibid.*
81. *Ibid.*
82. Alexander von Humboldt, *Kosmos. Entwurf einer physischen Weltbeschreibung,* 5 vols. (J. G. Cotta, Stuttgart and Tübingen, 1845–1862), Vol. I, p. 6.
83. Teilhard de Chardin, *The Phenomenon of Man,* p. 11.
84. *Ibid.,* pp. 284f.
85. *Ibid.,* p. 295.
86. *Ibid.,* p. 297.
87. Pierre Teilhard de Chardin, *Letters to Léontine Zanta* (Harper & Row, 1968), p. 61.